WEB
DESIGN

START HERE ▶

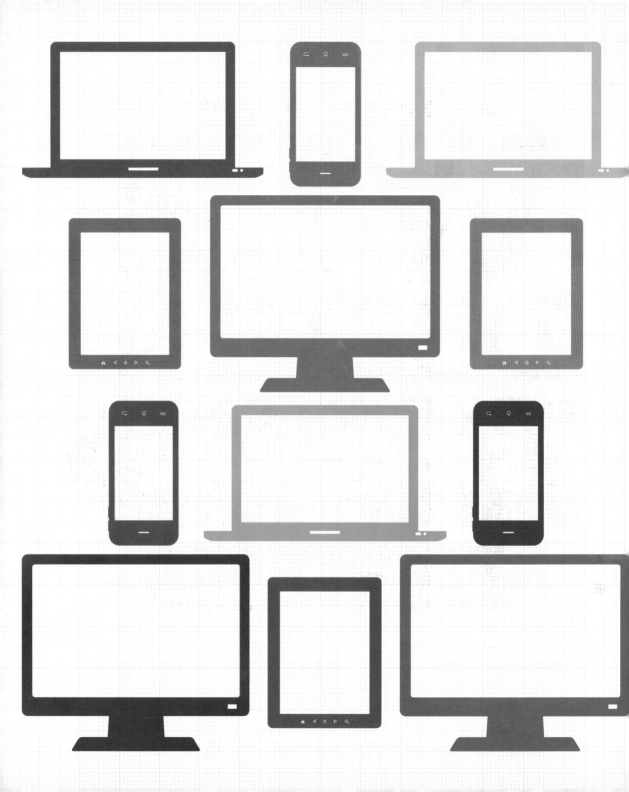

STEFAN MISCHOOK

WEB DESIGN

START HERE ▶

A No-Nonsense, Jargon-Free Guide to the Fundamentals of Web Design

HOW
BOOKS

CINCINNATI, OHIO
WWW.HOWDESIGN.COM

Published in the United States by
HOW Books, an imprint of
F+W Media, Inc., 10151 Carver Road,
Suite 200, Blue Ash, Ohio 45242.
(800) 289-0963. First edition.

For more excellent books and resources for designers,
visit www.howdesign.com

16 15 14 13 12   5 4 3 2 1

ISBN-13: 978-1-4403-4112-0

This book was conceived, designed, and produced by
The ILEX Press,
a division of Octopus Publishing Group Ltd
Octopus Publishing Group
Carmelite House
50 Victoria Embankment
London, EC4Y 0DZ
www.octopusbooks.co.uk

Executive Publisher: Roly Allen
Senior Specialist Editor: Frank Gallaugher
Senior Project Editor: Natalia Price-Cabrera
Assistant Editor: Rachel Silverlight
Commissioning Editor: Zara Larcombe
Art Director: Julie Weir
Designer: Kate Haynes
Senior Production Manager: Peter Hunt

a content + ecommerce company

PART 2:

WEB-DESIGN TOOLKIT

Introduction

This book is about code and cutting-edge web design. It starts off with the big picture, and then slowly circles in for the web design kill! I won't leave you hanging with just a bunch of nerd-code either, not knowing what to do with it—no, no, no! Instead, not only will you learn how to build a modern website, you will also learn how to get it live on the web.

Web design in 2015 and beyond

Today web design has become much more sophisticated, and requires a skill set that is very much different from graphic design. Yes, the pages in your websites should look good, but that's only a small part of what makes a professional website these days.

Learning to code is the key to web design

In the last couple of years there has been a worldwide awakening with regards to the importance of learning to code. As such, I will concentrate on the coding end of things.

How this book is structured

I've divided this book into two sections. The first half of the book is largely a step-by-step tutorial where you jump straight away into building a simple website. Along the way I will introduce you to key web design concepts, while intermixing practical techniques as you continue to build out your very first website.

You must follow the steps!

It's important that in the first half of the book you follow the tutorials in proper order, as each chapter builds off the ones that precede it (except for Chapter 1, of course!). So, if you skipped Chapter 2 and jumped to Chapter 3 you would miss some important information.

The second half of the book is the Toolbox, which is where it gets fun! Here you have the freedom to jump around as you learn a bunch of cool web design techniques. The Toolbox will take your skills to the next level of nerd goodness.

You will be covering a lot of material in this book and I encourage you to write out the code as you go, as this will help you with the learning process. However, although I've worked hard to make this book easy to understand, there might be times when things don't seem to work. No worries about that! Just visit the book's website for all the source files, and links to supplementary videos. You can even ask me questions directly!

Thanks!
Stefan Mischook

Companion website

Download source files for each chapter and access supplementary material from the book's companion website:

http://www.webdesignstarthere.com

CHAPTER 1

Getting Started in Web Design

Just about everybody uses the web these days—even my little old granny! But how is the web put together? And why should you care?

In this chapter we will look under the digital hood and explore some core concepts that are important to the way the web works.

Why the overview? I've found over the years that it's a lot easier to learn web design if you first have a bird's-eye view of things.

The first thing we should cover is the gear you will need and the ideal setup I would recommend—not only when learning web design, but when you are out there in the real world building websites.

What is the best computer for web design?

First of all, you can use any old crappy computer and it will be more than powerful enough to start building amazing websites. If you think about it, web design is largely about writing code—this is just text and even your old iPhone can write lots of text! I am not saying you should be building websites on your iPhone (but you know what, that might be coming in the next couple of years).

A good monitor is a big plus

If you can afford it, get yourself a nice monitor—it's just easier to work with and you will be more productive. Nicer means bigger and with more pixels, and of course flat panel.

Laptop or desktop?

The best thing to have is a laptop and an external flat panel display to hook it up to when you are at your desk. A laptop is great because you can move around with it, visit clients, and show them how the progress is going with their website—it just gives you that flexibility.

That said, an old desktop with a CRT monitor is fine—many fantastic websites have been designed on these.

SSD storage

SSD is short for "solid-state drive" and it is a type of storage that's a couple orders of magnitude faster than traditional hard drives. I highly recommend that you get a computer (laptop or desktop) with SSD storage because it will speed things up like crazy. My two-year-old SSD-based ultra-thin laptop can boot up Windows 7 cold in nine seconds, while my MacBook Pro SSD boots in about 12 seconds!

Powerful processors are not too important in web design

When people think of computer speed, they always think of the CPU—2.9 GHz Intel Core i7, etc. For web design, the speed of the computer is much more about the hard disk rather than the CPU. This is because you will be opening and closing a lot of files and the speed of this is all hard drive. Trust me, the few seconds that you save each time you open files

and apps adds up at the end of the day. In short, web design is hard drive intensive and hardly ever CPU intensive. If you have the money, get an SSD-based computer. My favorites are the MacBook Air and the Samsung Ativ Book, but any SSD-based computer will rock!

High-speed internet

The internet is like a car: the faster the better. Being able to upload and download files in a flash just feels good. When you are searching for specific tips on how to do something on Google, speed is essential!

If you can afford it and it is available in your part of the world, get it. Even my father's got high-speed internet—and he's really old!

Basic concepts of the web

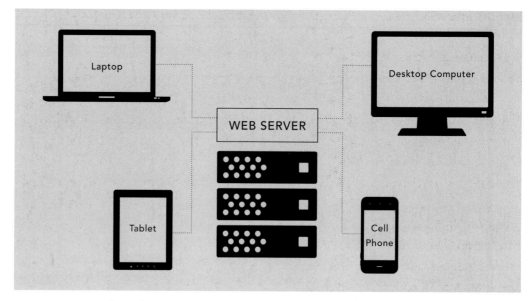

The web is a network of interconnected computers all linked up to a web server.

I assume that you know nothing about the inner workings of the internet; maybe you're not even sure how people get to websites, where the websites are actually sitting, and what the web even is in the first place.

Over the next few pages I am going to give you the minimum you need to "get your feet wet," so you can quickly get into building websites. I won't go into painful micro-detail—rather, I'll give you just enough so that you have a basic understanding. This is important, because it provides you with a "map" that will make learning web design easier.

What is the web?

In a nutshell, the web is a whole bunch of interconnected computers talking to one another. The computers (on the web) are typically connected by phone lines, satellite signals, cable TV lines, and other types of data-transfer mechanisms. A "data-transfer mechanism" is a nerd's way of saying a way to move information from point A to point B to point C, and so on.

The computers that make up the web can be connected all the time (24/7), or only periodically. The computers that are connected all the time are typically called "servers." Servers are computers just like any home computer, with one major difference: they have special "server software" installed.

Server software is created to "serve" web pages and websites. Basically, the server has a bunch of websites loaded on it and it just waits for people (via web browsers) to request or ask for a particular page. When the web browser requests a page the server sends it out.

How does the web surfer find a website?

The short answer is by typing in a URL, or in other words, a website "address." For example, if you wanted to find the website www.killersites.com, you would type that address into your web browser's address bar or use a "Favorites" or "Bookmarks" link to go to Killersites.

There are other ways to find websites (such as using a search engines), but behind the scenes websites are all being found by going to the website's official address. That brings us to our last detail: how does a website get an official address so that the rest of the web can find it?

When a web browser requests a web page (on a tablet, cell phone, or computer), the server sends it out.

Domains & servers

What's a domain name?

The previous page probably gave you an idea about what registering a domain was all about. But just in case, registering a domain name gets you an "official" address for your website on the world wide web. With this official address, the rest of the web can find you.

Just as your home address is unique in the real world, there also can't be any duplicate addresses on the internet, otherwise no one would know where to go! In other words, domain names are unique addresses on the web.

Why it costs money to register a domain name

If you want to have your own unique address on the web—your own domain name—it will cost a few bucks for each year you want to "own" the name. The cost of registering a domain name ranges from less than $10 USD to about $30 USD per year. You can register a domain from one to ten years.

The reason for the cost is that the central "address book" of all the world's domain names needs to be updated—and somebody's got to pay for that! You

may have noticed that I just snuck in a little extra piece of information: the giant "web address book" of domains.

This leads us to our last bit of information: when you type in a website's domain name or click on a link that takes you to that domain name, your browser starts asking servers where on the web that particular domain name is sitting. The servers can then tell the browser where to go, by referring to the giant address book I mentioned above.

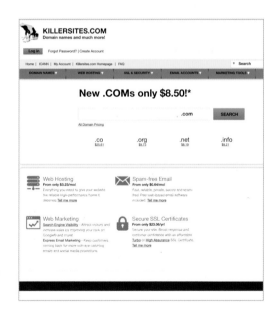

Hosting.killersites.com is one of many, many websites where you can register a domain. (In the interest of transparency, this is my site.)

Getting your website "live" on the web

With the background details under your belt, you can now learn about the two steps to going live on the web: registering your domain and renting server space.

Registering your domain

There are many companies out there that allow you to register the domain name for your website. Prices vary, as does the quality of service, but at the end of the day they all handle the details of getting your domain name listed in the giant address book.

These days, you will find that many of the names you may be interested in registering are already taken. This means you will likely have to be creative (and patient) to come up with a good domain.

Renting server space

You need to rent space on a server so that it can serve your website to the web: this is called "hosting." Companies that provide this service are called "hosts" or hosting companies.

After you've registered your domain, you need to set up an account with a hosting company and tell them your

What is the difference between .com, .net, .org, and so on?

Practically speaking, there is really no difference these days. Search engines don't discriminate between a .com address and (for example) a .net address. The only thing you might consider is that people tend to type in .com automatically since it was the first publicly known domain extension. So, when registering a domain name I would go for the .com first and if it is taken I would then try for any of the others (.net, .org, .tv, and so on).

You probably guessed from this that a .com address is not the same as another domain with the same name, but different extension. For example, www.killersites.com is not the same place as www.killersites.net. As such, each address will need to be registered separately.

domain name—you'll also need to assign your host's "nameservers" to the domain name (see the box below). After this, you should be live on the web typically within a week, or less.

Moving your website files onto the server

After you have registered your domain name and have your hosting service in place, the final step is to upload your website onto the server.

You can transfer your website to your host's server using an FTP program. An FTP program is a type of software that is used to move files from one computer to another over the internet. FTP is the acronym for "file transfer protocol," which is just nerd-speak that describes a way of

Nameservers

Nameservers are servers that manage the location of all the domains on the web. When you register a domain you will be asked to assign a nameserver to the domain—each hosting company has their own. You don't have to do it at that moment, but you will have to do it before your site can be seen on the web. Your hosting company will let you know which nameservers to use.

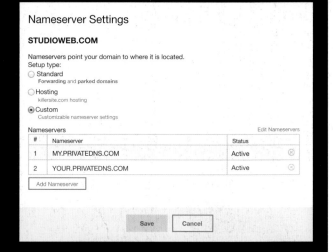

You set your domain's DNS (nameservers) in a control panel at the registrar where you registered your domain.

FTP

WEB SERVER

Website files are uploaded to your host's server using an FTP program.

A cheaper option to getting your site online?

Some people may not want to buy a domain or pay for hosting because they only have a personal website for fun or practice. You can still get your website live on the web by using a free hosting service that allows you to create a "subdomain." A subdomain is just a domain that is part of another domain. So, if killersites.com offered subdomain hosting, you would be able to have an address like this:
http://yourwebsite.killersites.com

What you need to understand here is that your website's domain is really just a part of the parent domain. Doing it this way, you don't need to buy a domain name, and you typically don't need to pay for hosting.

This is fine for fun or project websites, but if you are serious about your website (say it's your business website), using a subdomain is like taking someone else's business card and writing your name on it!

One last point. I've heard of free hosting services that will allow you to host proper domains with them for free, and without the annoying ads that other free hosts will insert into your pages. But I've never used them, and in my experience you tend to get what you pay for.

moving files (a "protocol" is just a certain way of doing things).

There are several free FTP programs you can use to move your files. For example, FireZilla is a free FTP app that will run on both Windows and Mac OS. I've used it and it works pretty well. You can download it here: https://filezilla-project.org/download.php.

Another option you have to "FTP" your files to the server is to simply use your web browser. All the major browsers either have FTP capabilities built into them, or they have free add-on or plugin FTP programs you can download and install as additions. (We call them "plugins" because they plug into the web browser.)

The Firefox and Chrome web browsers make it easy to access your files by FTP: all you have to do is type your server's FTP address into the web browser's address bar—as is the example ftp://studioweb.com shown opposite (1).

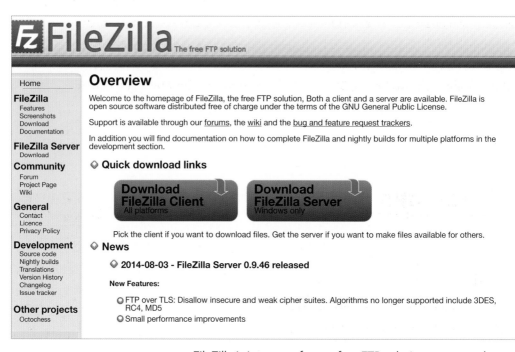

FileZilla is just one of many free FTP solutions you can choose. Once upon a time, we used to pay good money for these!

Index of ftp://studioweb.com/

📁 Up to higher level directory

Name	Size	Last Modified
.bash_logout	1 KB	2012-05-10 12:00:00 AM
.bash_profile	1 KB	2012-05-10 12:00:00 AM
.bashrc	1 KB	2012-05-10 12:00:00 AM
.contactemail		2012-07-04 12:00:00 AM
.cpaddons		2012-08-07 12:00:00 AM
.cpanel		2013-08-19 4:38:00 PM
.ftpquota	1 KB	2013-08-11 5:08:00 AM
.htpasswds		2012-07-04 12:00:00 AM
.lastlogin	1 KB	2013-05-31 6:49:00 PM
access-logs		2010-07-06 12:00:00 AM
cpbackup-exclude.conf	1 KB	2008-12-18 12:00:00 AM
cpmove.psql		2010-07-06 12:00:00 AM
cpmove.psql.1278442379		2008-02-29 12:00:00 AM
etc		2011-01-07 12:00:00 AM
logs		2007-08-11 12:00:00 AM
mail		2008-12-17 12:00:00 AM
public		2013-03-21 11:35:00 PM
public_ftp		2011-01-08 12:00:00 AM
public_html		2011-01-07 12:00:00 AM
root_print.css		2007-05-24 12:00:00 AM
ssl		2013-06-17 10:49:00 AM

Authentication Required

Enter username and password for ftp://studioweb.com

User Name:

Password:

Cancel   OK

Once logged in, you will see a list of the files in your server space, as you can see in the screenshot above right (2). To upload, you need to add a plugin—for example, FireFTP for Firefox; add it here: https://addons.mozilla.org/en-US/firefox/addon/fireftp/ (shown below, 3).

Whoa! We've covered the basic concepts!

I like having a general understanding of things before I jump into the dirty details, and that's exactly what we've just done in this chapter. Now you're ready to learn how to build a web page.

ADD-ONS

EXTENSIONS | THEMES | COLLECTIONS | MORE...

🏠 » Extensions » FireFTP

FireFTP *2.0.19*
by Mime Cuvalo

Fire FTP is a free, secure, cross-platform FTP/SFTP client for Mozilla Firefox which provides easy and intuitive access to FTP/SFTP servers.

Check out my new project, FireSHH!

FEATURED

★★★★★

Add to collection

Share this Add-on

The FireFTP plugin is actually installed inside the Firefox web browser.

Building your first web page

There are three ways that you can build a web page: you can either use a pre-made template, use a WYSIWYG app, or hand code your HTML.

1. Use a pre-made template

A website template is a pre-made website that can be customized any way you like—assuming you have the web design skills. These templates are typically supplied in HTML format, but sometimes you can get them as a Photoshop file—in which case it is expected that you will know how to use Photoshop to create the website.

Website templates can be very useful; they can be used by experienced web designers to jump-start the creation of a website. They are also a way for people to put out great-looking websites quickly with little or no design skills.

2. Use a WYSIWYG web design app like Dreamweaver

WYSIWYG is short for "What You See Is What You Get." These are apps that allow you to point-and-click and drag-and-drop your way to building a web page. What the WYSIWYG app displays as you build your web page is pretty close to what it would look like on the web.

WYSIWYG web design apps make building web pages similar to creating a document in, say, Microsoft Word or Photoshop. It seems pretty easy, but even with WYSIWYG apps, you still need to understand the code behind your pages.

Beyond that, there is a downside to only using WYSIWYG apps—you can lose a certain amount of control with what you're doing and in some cases, you can become dependent on the app.

3. Hand code your HTML with a simple text editor or a code editor

That means you type in the HTML code yourself. This is the approach we are going to use here, because it's the quickest way to learn how to build websites.

Hand-coding HTML is also the best way because you have the most control over what you're doing. Besides, once you understand the code behind the web pages you will find that you can work as fast or faster than you would using a WYSIWYG app like Dreamweaver.

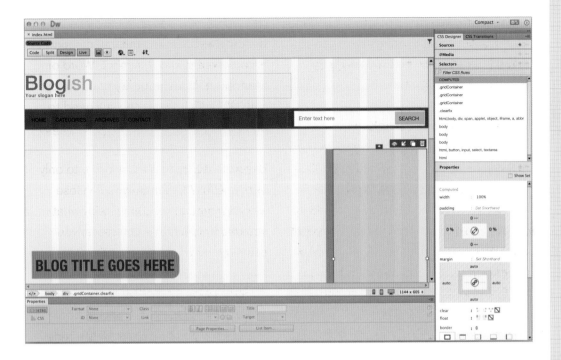

Adobe Dreamweaver CC is now offered only as a subscription.

Don't get me wrong—I am not saying using WYSIWYG web design software is necessarily a bad idea. What you will find, though, is that with a little experience even those who use WYSIWYG software tend to use the code editing part of the app the most.

Code editors vs. simple text editors

Simple text editors include programs such as Notepad on Windows (1) and TextEdit on Mac (2). These programs are no-frills text editors that can be used to create web pages. I wouldn't use rich text editors like MS Word or Apple's Pages because these apps can insert extra formatting into the pages that will give you headaches.

❶

❷

Code editors on the other hand, are apps specifically designed to assist you in writing code. They make it easier to write code with built-in code coloring that makes the code easier to read, line numbering along the left side of the page (line numbers help a lot with organizing code on a page) and a whole bunch of other stuff.

Fortunately, there are many code editors out there that are either free or very inexpensive; Sublime Text (3), which works on both Windows and Mac OS, is very popular these days. You can download a demo at http://www.sublimetext.com.

Alternatively, you can try the Windows-only Notepad++ (4) from http://notepad-plus-plus.org/download/v6.6.9.html or the Mac-only TextWrangler (5), which is available from Apple's App Store.

Today, many professional web designers and developers use code editors rather than WYSIWYG apps. I don't know what the exact percentages are, but the trend is definitely in the direction of using code editors. If you want to get work in web design today, you need to know code!

OK, now that we know the advantages of hand-coding web pages, let's look at the bare minimum of theory needed.

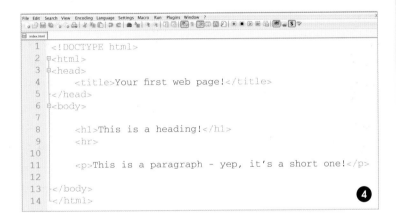

What are HTML tags?

HTML tags are specifically formatted text elements that create "markers" for web browsers to read and interpret. These markers tell web browsers what to display on the web page and how to display it. Tags are placed in and around the text that you want to have appear in your web pages.

HTML has a whole bunch of tags (just like the alphabet has a whole bunch of letters) that the web designer can use to build web pages. Tags have a specific structure, so that when the browser is reading an HTML page it can differentiate tags from normal text.

Tags are typically words or abbreviations of words placed between angled brackets. To make text bold, for example, HTML uses the "bold" tag:

```
<b>This text will be bold.</b>
```

Another commonly used tag is the paragraph tag:

```
<p>This is a paragraph of text.</p>
```

You may have noticed that HTML tags come in pairs: typically (though not always—we'll see that later) HTML has both an opening tag (<tag name>) and a closing tag (</tag name>). The only difference between the opening and closing tags is that a closing tag contains an extra forward slash.

Here are a few examples of HTML tags:

```
<b>Makes text bold.</b>
<i>Makes text italic.</i>
<h1>Tells the browser that this
text is very important—the browser
usually makes this text really
big.</h1>
```

HTML tags are not just for placing and formatting text; HTML tags can be used to include other things like images, video, audio, and even multimedia programs.

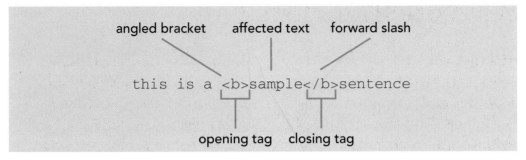

this is a samplesentence

angled bracket   affected text   forward slash

opening tag   closing tag

HTML opening and closing tags—here, the word "sample" will display in bold.

Comparing HTML code and the web page it creates

Let's start with a very simple web page to make it easy for you to understand. First let's look at the final page (1).

Now that we've seen what the page looks like, let's look at the HTML code used to create the page (2).

Take a little time and compare the webpage and the code used to create it. Notice where the HTML tags are, and what they are doing.

```
1  <!DOCTYPE html>
2  <html>
3  <head>
4          <title>Your first web page!</title>
5  </head>
6  <body>
7
8          <h1>This is a heading!</h1>
9          <hr>
10
11         <p>This is a paragraph - yep, it's a short one!</p>
12
13 </body>
14 </html>
```

The structure of an HTML page

An HTML page is divided into two major sections: the head and the body.

1. The head

The head (<head>) section contains underlying information about the page that does not get displayed in the web page (except for the title of the page). It does, however, have an affect on how the web page is displayed.

2. The body

The body (<body>) section contains all the stuff that appears on the actual web page when someone happens to come along with their web browser. We are talking about the actual text, images, video, and so on that people will see. That, of course, means the tags used to format all this stuff are here too.

You will notice that both the head and the body sections of a website are marked in the HTML page with their respective tags: (<head> </head>) and (<body> </body>).

If the body tag creates the body of an HTML page, and the head tag creates the head of an HTML page, how do you create an HTML page itself? You guessed it, use the HTML tags:

```
<html></html>
```

The "mother of all tags" is the HTML (<html>) tag, and like most other tags it must have a start tag (<html>) and an end tag (</html>). The difference between the start and end tags is the forward slash (/), but you already knew that.

Every web page must begin and end with the HTML tag, otherwise the web browser will not be able to display the page. You also have to have <head> tags and <body> tags. All other tags are optional.

So a bare-bones HTML page must have these tags, in this order:

```
<html>
<head>
<title>Title of your page</title>
</head>
<body>
</body>
</html>
```

Doctypes & web browser rendering engines

I just want to quickly cover something called the "doctype." The doctype (or "document-type") is a snippet of HTML code that you have to place at the very top of the page. It looks like this:

```
<!DOCTYPE html>
```

The doctype basically tells the web browser how to read and process your HTML page. There are other doctypes out there, and you will probably find them in older websites, for example:

```
<!DOCTYPE HTML PUBLIC "-//W3C//DTD
HTML 4.01//EN" "http://www.w3.org/
TR/html4/strict.dtd">
<!DOCTYPE HTML PUBLIC "-//W3C//DTD
HTML 4.01 Transitional//EN"
"http://www.w3.org/TR/html4/loose.
dtd">
```

And there are others!

Why so many doctypes? In a nutshell: web browsers have several built-in engines that are used to process HTML and CSS code; the doctype code simply tells the browser which one to use. To be clear,

each of these "engines" can interpret your code in slightly different ways, and this can lead to all kinds of headaches (for example pages not looking the same) especially with CSS code.

There is a long story behind all these different engines, but all you need to know is that that you should use the simple doctype:

```
<!DOCTYPE html>
```

This is the most modern doctype used by all web browsers, so it will tell the web browser to use the most modern engine.

How about not including a doctype—what happens? If you don't put in a doctype at the top of your page, the browser will use an old default engine (called "quirks mode"), which will probably screw up your web pages. So, if you want your web pages to look the same on all modern browsers, you need to add the doctype!

Building your first HTML page by hand

I could go on with more theory and send half of you to sleep—trust me! instead you are now actually going to build your very first web page. One of the best ways to learn something is to go on and do it, so don't worry if things are a little foggy for you right now; as you build the web page, things will start to clear up.

So, let's write some HTML code.

Windows:

1. Go to your desktop and right-click, then select New -> Text Document (be sure you don't select "Rich Text Document"). This will create a text document on your desktop. Name it "webpage.txt" and type in the following code:

```
<!DOCTYPE html>
<html>
<head><title>Your first hand coded
page</title>
</head>
<body>
<h2>Hand coding web pages is easy!
</h2>
```

```
<p>I would like to thank everyone
who helped me type this page.</p>
</body>
</html>
```

2. Go to File -> Save As and in the "File name" box, name it "webpage.html" (1). This will create a separate HTML page on your desktop with the icon of your default browser (2). For me, this is Google Chrome.

You can choose any name you want, as long as you follow these rules:

• Web page names cannot have spaces in them: "web page.html" is no good but "webpage.html" is perfecto.

Download the files

Don't forget that you can download the code files for every exercise in this book by visiting the book's website at **http://www.webdesignstarthere.com.**

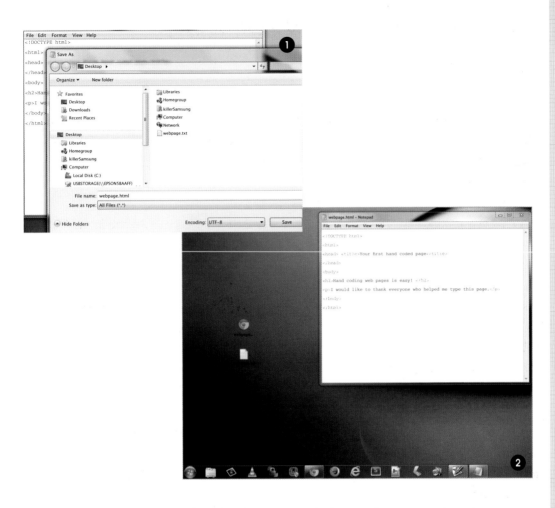

- The name has to end with the ".html" extension; by ending the filename this way you are telling the computer that this is a web page and it should use a web browser to view it.

- Don't use funny symbols such as $, %, ^, or & in your page names. Stick to standard letters and numbers—using a dash or underscore is also ok. For example: web-page.html and web_page.html are good. (Yes, many strange characters will work in technical terms, but having clean page names avoids any confusions.)

- Select an Encoding of UTF-8.

Showing filename extensions in Windows

Some of you may have Windows set up to not show the file extensions—this means you will not see the .html or the .txt of your text document. You will need to make a small change to Windows to see the file extensions. Follow these steps:

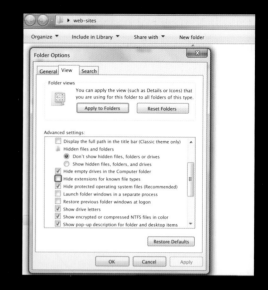

Windows Vista & Windows 7

1. Start Windows Explorer; you can do this by opening up any folder.

2. Click Organize.

3. Click Folder and search options.

4. Click the View tab.

5. Scroll down until you see "Hide extensions for known file types" (as shown above right); uncheck this line by clicking the check box.

6. Click OK.

Windows 8.1

1. Open Windows Explorer and select the View tab.

2. Click the Options button and select "Change folder and search options."

3. Click the View tab.

4. Scroll down until you see "Hide extensions for known file types" (looks like Windows 7, above); uncheck this line by clicking the check box.

5. Click OK.

Mac:

1. Launch TextEdit and create a new document (File -> New).

2. Select Format -> Make Plain Text.

3. Enter this code:

```
<html>
<head>
<title>Your first hand coded page
</title>
</head>
<body>
<h2>Hand coding web pages is easy!
</h2>
<p>I would like to thank everyone
who helped me type this page.</p>
</body>
</html>
```

4. Select File -> Save, or use your keyboard and press Command + S.

5. Save the file onto your desktop as "index.html"(1).

6. You will be asked if you want to use ".html"; do that (2).

Windows & Mac:

Marvel at your work! Just double-click on the page or open it up with your web browser by going to its "File" menu, choosing Open File, and then selecting your page.

You should be able to see your page in all its glory (3)! OK, there's not too much glory, but it was your first hand-coded page after all. If you don't see anything, then compare what you typed with the original code and go over the process again. You will get it if you give yourself a chance!

Some notes on HTML tags

HTML tags are not case sensitive: <P> or <p> both work. Using lowercase tags is just easier to read.

The white space between tags is not important and will not effect how your pages look.

So this page of roughly formatted HTML code:

```
<html>

        <head>
                <title>Your first
hand coded page</title>
        </head>
        <body>
                <h2>Hand coding web
pages is easy! </h2>
                <p>I would like to
thank everyone who helped me
type this page.</p>
        </body>
</html>
```

… will look exactly the same as this page of code when it is viewed in a web browser:

```
<html>
<head>
<title>Your first hand coded
page</title>
</head>
<body><h2>Hand coding web pages
is easy!</h2><p>I would like to
thank everyone who helped me
type this page.</p>
</body>
</html>
```

However, it is much easier to read and write HTML code that is nicely formatted!

As we have said, HTML tags typically have an opening and closing tag, but there are some exceptions, the most important being the <img> (image) tag. We will learn about these later.

Using a code editor

With all that talk about code editors near the beginning of the chapter you may be wondering where they fit in. You see, I got so excited to get you writing some code that I decided to just use the simple text editors built into Mac or Windows.

Going forward, it makes sense to use a proper code editor, because regardless of whichever one you choose, it will make your life much easier as you write code. Now is a good time to download one of the programs I suggested on page 20.

Once you've installed your code editor, you will automatically be able to choose it to open (and edit) a web page. For example, with the page you just created, right-click on it on your desktop and you will have the option to open it with your editor (1, below). In this instance I am using Sublime Text (2).

So what's next?

Linking some pages together and actually building your first proper website!

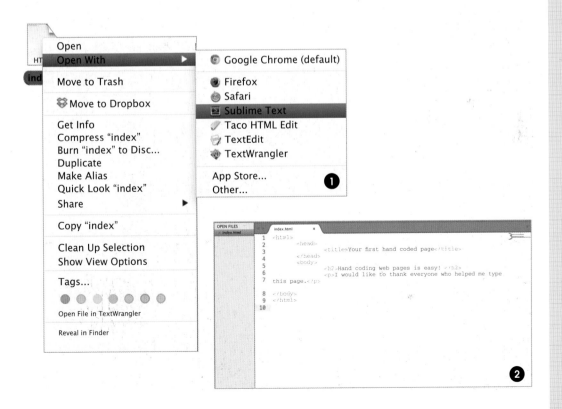

CHAPTER 2

Building a Website

Now that you have some of the basics of web design down, let's flesh out that knowledge and see how you can put it into practice and build your first website.

As with Chapter 1, the goal here is not to expose you to every tag, concept, and detail about web design—that would make your head explode! Instead, I am going to cover the basic components, so you come away with a solid foundation that you can use in the rest of the book.

Babysteps!

Don't worry, what you are learning gets more cool, the more we progress.

What is a website?

A website is just a bunch of web pages connected together by a thing called a "hyperlink." In HTML there is a special tag called the <a> tag, which creates hyperlinks. In its most basic form it looks like this:

```
<a href="..."></a>
```

(Note: I used "…" as a placeholder.)

You'd figure that the tag that is used to create links in web pages would be called the link tag, but nope, it's called the <a> tag. There is a link tag, but that's used for something else!

Anyway, here is an example of the <a> tag (hyperlink tag) with a destination (where you want the link to go to) filled in:

```
<a href="http://www.studioweb.
com">Go to studioweb.com.</a>
```

Tag attributes

You may have noticed the text "href=" in the <a> tag. This is an example of something called a "tag attribute." Tag attributes give you extra information about a tag. However, not all HTML tags have attributes and some of the attributes are optional. In other words, HTML tag attributes are attributes of tags, just like eye color, hair color and foot size are attributes of humans.

I guess an optional attribute of a human, might be, say, hair. At least that's where I'm going as I get older!

In the case of the <a> tag, the "href" tag attribute tells the web browser what to link to. In this example, it's to a website. It could also be to videos, images, audio, and more. You obviously need to include an "href" tag attribute if you want the hyperlink to go somewhere!

Here's another example of a tag attribute—"lang"—which can also be applied to the <html> tag:

```
<html lang="en-US">
```

Links vs. hyperlinks

In the nerd tech-spec, hyperlinks and links are not the same. In fact, they are two different tags: <a> and <link>. But in day-to-day web talk, people rarely say "Click on that hyperlink." No, we typically say "Click on the link." Therein lies the confusion. Just keep in mind that links and hyperlinks are not the same in code, or in what they do.

Just in case you are curious, we use <link> tags to link, or connect, other types of documents to our HTML pages. The only time I've ever used <link> tags is to connect to something called a CSS page (CSS is the sister language to HTML and is used to add style to a website—we will get into that more in the chapters on CSS). I can't think of any other use of <link>, so that probably means that you will never use the <link> tag for anything else!

The <a> tag or hyperlink

We have all used links (hyperlinks) when surfing the web. Whenever you click on a link that takes you to another page, you are using an <a> tag.

The hyperlink tag (<a>) is the most important tag in HTML because it makes the internet interconnected.

In the example on page 32, you saw that the hyperlink link tag points to the website www.studioweb.com and the text that is displayed on the web page is: "Go to studioweb.com." So, if you wanted to create a link that took someone to www.yahoo.com, for example, you would replace "www.studioweb.com" with "www.yahoo.com."

Like most other tags, hyperlink tags have an opening tag (<a href="http://www.studioweb.com">) and a closing tag (</a>). Hyperlink tags are a little more complex than the other tags we have seen so far, but I think that you can handle it!

Some of you may have noticed that there is some text in the hyperlink tag that comes before the website address; the text I am talking about is this:

```
http://
```

This text tells the browser how it should get the web page. It's pretty intricate stuff that only web programmers need to know, so don't worry about it for now. Sometimes links can point to other things besides web pages, such as videos, MP3 files, PDF files, and so on.

Absolute vs. relative URLs

To link pages in your website from one page to the next, you have a choice of using one of two types of addresses: absolute addresses (complete) and relative addresses (partial).

Before I go on, "URL" is a nerd's way of saying "address."

Absolute URLs

An absolute URL is the complete address of a page that can be found from any other location on the internet. Let's say you have a page called contact.html on the root of your website, whose domain name is "www.webmentor.org." In this case, the absolute URL of the contact.html page would be:

http://www.webmentor.org/contact.html

OK, now I know I lost a few people because I used a word that I haven't explained yet: "root."

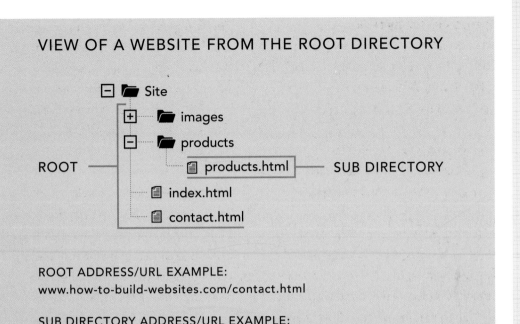

VIEW OF A WEBSITE FROM THE ROOT DIRECTORY

ROOT ——

- ⊟ 📁 Site
  - ⊞ 📁 images
  - ⊟ 📁 products
    - 📄 products.html —— SUB DIRECTORY
  - 📄 index.html
  - 📄 contact.html

ROOT ADDRESS/URL EXAMPLE:
www.how-to-build-websites.com/contact.html

SUB DIRECTORY ADDRESS/URL EXAMPLE:
www.how-to-build-websites.com/products/products.html

When geeks talk about the root of a website, they are talking about the base of the website; the starting level.

The files (pages, images, and so on) that make up your website are organized into folders, just like any other files that you store on your home computer. Your host will give you a space or directory on their server where you will place all your website's files.

The space or folder assigned to you will be the "root" of your website. This means that as far as the internet is concerned, anything in this folder (html files, images, other folders, and so on) is directly accessible by your domain name plus the name of the item.

For example, let's say that on the root level of your website you had these HTML files: index.html and contact.html. Now, in a folder called "products" you place a whole bunch of other pages, including one called "bookcases.html." You decided to put all your "product" HTML pages into a "products" folder to keep the website more organized—a smart thing to do!

Can you guess what the absolute URL would be for the web page "bookcases. html?" For the domain name "www. webmentor.org" it would be:

http://www.webmentor.org/products/ bookcases.html

Just think about it a little and hopefully it will sink in! If it doesn't right away, don't worry, it will come.

Relative URLs

A relative URL is a partial address that is relative to the page where you placed your hyperlink. So if you were linking from the index.html page of this website to the bookcases.html page, your relative URL (address) would be:

```
products/bookcases.html
```

And the actual hyperlink tag would look like this:

```
<a href="products/bookcases.
html">Check out our bookcases!</a>
```

You are basically telling the browser that the HTML page we want to load is in the products folder. Play around with hyperlinks and folders on your own website and things will become very

clear. This is important because if you get the address wrong, it won't load!

OK, say you wanted to link to "contact. html" from the "index.html" page:

```
<a href="contact.html">Contact us
</a>
```

Since the page "contact.html" is on the same level as the page "index.html," we need only include the name of the html file in the hyperlink address.

Linking to a site root page with relative links

Let's say you wanted to link back to the site root (with a relative link) from a page in a sub folder. Looking back at the diagram on the previous page, I would use this link on the products page to get us back to the root contact.html page:

```
<a href="../contact.html">to
contact page</a>
```

This code (../) tells the web browser to go up one level in the directory hierarchy. If I wanted to go up two levels (in the site hierarchy) you would use ../ twice:

```
<a href="../../contact.html">to
contact page</a>
```

The process of creating a website

Now that we've got some preliminary theory out of the way (it's about time) we can go over the 10 steps you'll need to take to build and make a website "live" on the web.

1. Define the purpose of the website

When starting a website project you must first clarify what the goals of the website are. Knowing your goals will affect the choices you make when putting the website together and ultimately contribute to its success or failure.

This may sound obvious, but many websites seem to have been put together without the goal kept in mind. The result is a messy website that is disorganized and harder to build and maintain.

If, for example, the goal is to create an e-commerce website that sells products, then as a website designer you would have to consider the following:

- Does the website need credit card processing capabilities?

- Are you going to need a shopping cart system to take orders?

- How many items will be listed/sold through the website?

This is just one example, but the point to take away is that by defining the purpose of the project you can better prepare and get the right tools or people for the job.

Purpose of website checklist

☐ Shopping cart?

☑ Contact form?

☐ Credit card processing?

☑ Blog capabilities?

☑ PayPal?

☑ Digital products?

Starting with a clear idea of the goals of the website will help you in the building process.

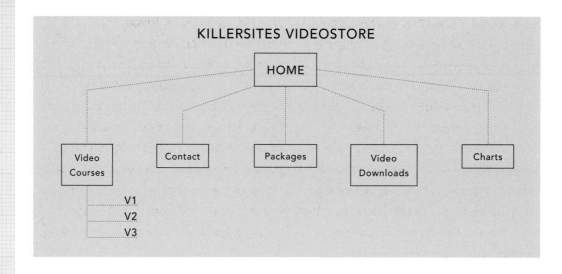

2. Structure the website

A simple diagram, as above, will help you (and your client if you have been hired to build a website) to visualize the site. You don't need anything special, just a series of boxes representing each page in the site with lines showing the linking strategy. A pyramid diagram is usually used to show the hierarchy of a website from the homepage down.

The homepage should always be called "index.html." I used the term "homepage" to indicate the first page that someone hits when they visit a website—it's a term that helps people understand the hierarchy of a website. So if you type "www.studioweb.com" in a web browser, the page that pops up is the homepage. In nerd reality, this "home page" is actually called the "index page."

A diagram of the structure of the website will help you work out the organization of the pages.

This is because web servers have a rule that on the root of any website, the page that it serves is the index.html page. If there is no index.html page, someone visiting your website won't see anything!

There are exceptions to that rule. For example, if you have a hosting account that runs PHP (PHP is a popular web programming language), web servers are configured in those cases to look first for "index.html" and if it can't find it, it will then try to load "index.php."

Exceptions aside, I would suggest that you name your homepage file: "index.html."

3. Write out the text for the website

Before you start writing any HTML, you should (in your favorite word processor) write out all the text that you need to include in the website. Doing so will help you with the design process.

Another thing you should do is to make sure that the text is finalized before it gets to the website; it is much easier to correct things in a word processor than in an HTML page.

4. Choose a basic layout that will be used on all pages

Armed with your website diagram and your text you can now choose a basic layout for your pages. You can go crazy with some funky artsy website (and sometimes it can work), but most of the time you should use standard layouts that people are used to—for example, a two-or three-column layout (below), or top navigation (over).

Two- or three-column layouts.
Refs: http://time.com;
http://cnn.com

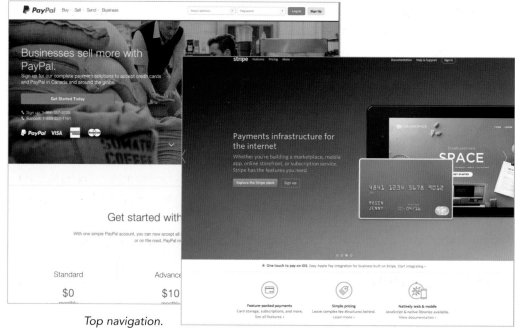

Top navigation.
Refs: http://paypal.com;
https://stripe.com

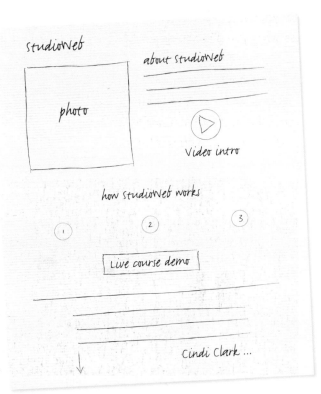

When in doubt, think of how books are laid out. As with the site diagram, you can use paper and pencil to play around with basic layout ideas for your pages before you get to coding—as in the example to the right.

Sketch out your page layout before starting to code.

5. Choose the basic color scheme and fonts for the site

Your next task is to start considering the basic colors and fonts that you're going to use. You want to choose a style that fits the subject of the website. For example, pink doesn't do well for a hardware store—maybe some steel blues instead!

Later on in the book I will teach you how to work with an easy-to-use technology that makes websites a breeze to style: CSS.

6. Build out the website

With steps 1–5 completed, you're ready to actually start creating the web pages for your very first site—aren't you excited! So what you need to do is:

• Create a folder somewhere on your computer that is easy to find (such as your desktop) and give it the name of the site that you want to build.

• Take the structure you developed in steps 1–5, and create the web pages in your website folder. Yes, the pages will be really, really simple since you haven't gotten to layouts and styling, but that doesn't matter. The goal here is to be able to hyperlink a bunch of pages together and write some basic code. As you write more and more HTML, you will slowly develop your "nerd" eyes.

• Link the web pages together.

Now is the time for you to practice a little and actually build a small website! If you can't think of something, create one on your favorite movie with a page for each of the main characters. Remember that you only get good at doing something by doing it!

Choosing colors for your site

Adobe has a free tool that helps you to chdoose complementary color schemes for your websites. You can check it out at: https://color.adobe.com/create/color-wheel.

7. Choose a domain name

Once your website is built, you will need to get it on the web—that means you need a domain name.

All websites need a domain name. Your choice of domain name can impact on how many people find your website, so choose carefully.

Domain names that tell you something about the website are "food" for search engines and they help clue people in too. If, for example, you were building a website for a hardware store, a domain name such as "discountHardware.com" is good because it tells you everything about the website immediately. However, if you called it "bigSteel.com" it's not giving such a clear message (although it is a short, memorable name, which also has its advantages).

Search engines such as Google will look at several elements of your website to try and determine what your website is about. One of those key elements is the domain name; Google will look for keywords in the domain name that help the "Google bot" (Google's automated snooper software) to categorize your website.

One question that is asked often is whether the domain name has to have the same name as the business it is representing—the answer is no.

8. Register your domain name

This can be trickier than you think, as many domain names are taken. You can pretty much forget single-word domain names like "business.com" and "auctions.com"—they are long gone! Instead, you will need to come up with combination names, such as "how-to-build-websites.com." I've spent days trying to find a good domain name!

That said, today you have many more options for domains because there are many more TLDs ("Top Level Domains"), such as .com, .net, .org, .biz, info, and .ws. That just scratches the surface—there are over 1000 new ones that have recently been made available!

If it is not clear, a TLD is basically the domain name extension. So with www.studioweb.com, the extension (and TLD) is ".com."

How do you know if a domain is already taken?

The quickest way to figure this out is to type the domain name into your browser and see if it takes you anywhere. This is not always useful though, because many domains have been bought, but have no website!

That means the best way to figure this out is to go to your registrar. Every registrar will have a form where you can check to see if domain names are available, just by typing it in.

The best thing about going to the registrar is that when you type a domain name you are interested in, its systems will not only tell you if the .com is available, but will also give you the scoop on all the other variations, which can be a big time saver.

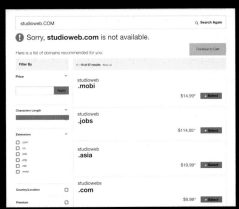

The first step in registering a domain name is to search for it!

What can affect the cost of hosting a website?

Traffic—more traffic can cost you more money per month. But for this to affect you, you would have to have a pretty popular website. For a brand new website, you wouldn't expect that problem for a while.

Extra features or services—you may need to use a database (for e-commerce), or need many email accounts or extra disk space to store all the website files. Each host will have a list of plans that you can choose from, depending on your, or your client's, needs (and budget).

In the end you have to choose the hosting company and hosting plan that is best suited to the website you're building. Cheaper is not always best, but it may sometimes be good enough.

9. Find a hosting company

Today, hosting a website costs much less than it did just a few years ago—competition is a good thing! You can go from zero-cost hosting to very pricey solutions, depending on your needs.

10. Upload your website to the hosting company's server

Once you've created your website, paid for your domain name, and set up your hosting, it's time to upload the website to the server for the world to see.

Typically, you would use FTP to do this (as we talked about in Chapter 1); your hosting company will provide the details when setting up your account.

A tip: with most hosting, your website files go into the "public_html" folder.

Name	Size	Last Modified (EDT)	Type	Perms
blog_images	4 KB	Jun 19, 2014 2:35 PM	httpd/unix-directory	0755
brew	4 KB	Jun 17, 2014 4.42 PM	httpd/unix-directory	0755
cgi-bin	4 KB	Jun 8, 2014 9.30 PM	httpd/unix-directory	0755
packages	4 KB	Jun 12, 2014 8:08 PM	httpd/unix-directory	0755
resources	4 KB	Jun 12, 2014 8:085 PM	httpd/unix-directory	0755
error_log	4 48 KB	Jun 13, 2014 8:25 PM	text/x-generic	0644
favicon.ico	1.12 KB	Jun 13, 2014 5:46	image/x-generic	0644

Some quick tips to remember

• Use descriptive page names that tell people (and search engines) what the page is about. For example: "products.html," "contact.html."

• People don't like to read long paragraphs of text on websites, so it is better to use shorter paragraphs, bulleted lists, and sub-headings.

• Keep contact information (email and phone) easily found in the same place on all pages.

• Keep the look and structure of your web pages consistent across the website.

• Provide a hyperlink back to the index page of the website. Many times, the website or company logo acts as this link.

Many hosting companies provide the cPanel file manager.

• Remember that you always have to have an index.html page on the root of your website—this is the homepage.

What's next?

Now that you've covered the basics of HTML and building a website we will start exploring CSS. As I've mentioned, this is the code used to make websites look good.

Finally, if you haven't tried creating a mini website, now is a good time do it—practice makes perfect!

CHAPTER 3

A Quick Introduction to CSS

So far we've been learning how to use HTML to create our basic web pages. But they lack style, pizazz and overall good looks—that's where CSS comes in!

CSS is one of the trickier parts of web design to learn. It's a tough nut to crack mentally at first, so don't worry if some of the concepts are hard to understand at the outset.

How's that for encouragement?!

What is CSS?

CSS is short for "Cascading Style Sheets." CSS is the sister language to HTML that allows you to style your web pages.

One example of a style change would be to make words look bold. In HTML you could use the <b> tag like so:

```
<b>Make me bold</b>
```

This works fine and there is nothing wrong with it, except that now, if you wanted to (for example) change all the text that you initially made bold to underline, you would have to go to every spot in every page, and swap the <b> tag for the underline tag.

CSS makes styling your websites much easier and it also makes it super easy to update the styles of pages—and websites are almost always in need of updates!

Here is another example of using old-school HTML to add style to your pages. To make text bold, set the font style to Verdana and change its color to red, you would need a lot of code around the text:

```
<font color="#FF0000"
face="Verdana, Arial, Helvetica,
sans-serif"><b>This is text</b>
</font>
```

- Videos
- Martha's Blog
- Martha's Pets
- American Made
- Weddings

- Cook
- Create
- Celebrate
- Shop
- Exclusive! Watch Martha Interview Blake Lively

Browse Topics By:

- Food
  - Classic Recipes
  - Key Ingredients
  - Basic Techniques
- Home Decorating
  - Room by Room
  - Furniture & Accents
  - DIY Home Decor
- Homekeeping
  - Get Organized
  - Cleaning & Care
- Gardening & Outdoors
  - Plants & Flowers
  - Outdoor Space
  - Gardening How-to
- DIY & Crafts
  - Crafting Techniques
  - Crafting Materials
- DIY Style & Beauty
  - DIY Clothing & Accesory Style Tips
  - Jewellery
  - Beauty
- Holidays & Parties
  - Halloween
  - Holidays
  - Parties
  - Entertaining Essentials
- Family & Pets
- Videos

Browse Topics

- Videos
- Martha's Blog
- Martha's Pets
- American Made

Marthastewart.com before CSS is applied to the page.

You can see how transformative CSS is in this screenshot—a plain list of text becomes a great looking page. Ref: http://www.marthastewart.com

This is verbose and starts to make your code messy.

Now, imagine that at some point you wanted to change the font in your website to, say, Google's new font, Open Sans. Once again, you would have to scour your web pages and change all the font tags—a big pain in the butt!

As an aside, you don't need to worry about understanding the bit of code at the left—as I said, this is old-school HTML and is something you will never use. I just wanted to demonstrate this point: don't use HTML to style your pages!

Some basic CSS concepts

Before you move forward with practical CSS examples, you need to learn a few basic CSS concepts.

CSS classes

There are a few ways to add CSS into your web pages, and as you go through the tutorial you will learn about them. One of the ways is with a CSS "class."

A CSS class is basically a bunch of CSS code placed inside a virtual container of CSS code (see the example coming up). You name that chunk of code and can apply it to the HTML tags in your page. Think of a CSS class as like a cookie cutter that can be used over and over in your web pages.

That's a lot to take in, I know. So let's just continue through the examples to help clear things up.

Applying CSS to a page

With CSS, you can create a custom style on your page, write out all its properties, and give it a unique name—the CSS class name. Once your CSS class is created, you can then "tag" your HTML to apply the class:

```
<p class="myNewStyle">My CSS styled
text</p>
```

Our new CSS class is called "myNewStyle."

Now, between the <head> and </head> tags at the top of your web page, you would insert this CSS code that defines the new class you just applied:

```
<style type="text/css">
.myNewStyle {
font-family: Verdana, Arial,
Helvetica, sans-serif;
font-weight: bold;
color: gray;
}
</style>
```

In this example, we include the style sheet code right in the page. Writing CSS code right in your page is fine for smaller projects, or in situations where the styles you're defining will only be used in a single page. But if you are going to be applying CSS code on multiple web pages in your website (as you will do 99% of the time), then you need a better way to apply your CSS code.

```
<!DOCTYPE html>
<html>
<head>
<title>Chapter 3: A Quick Introduction to CSS</title>
<meta http-equiv="Content-Type" content="text/html;
charset=iso-8859-1">

<style type="text/css">
.myNewStyle {font-family: Verdana, Arial, Helvetica, sans-serif;
font-weight: bold; color: gray;}
</style>

</head>

<body>

<h1>The Main Heading</h1>

<p class="myNewStyle">
My CSS styled text ... In web design and programming, we are
always trying to find ways to reduce the amount of code we are
writing because less code equals less mistakes and less work.
Yes, we all love less work!
</p>
</body>
</html>
```

A view of the page in code (or as we often say: "Code View").

The Main Heading

My CSS styled text ... In web design and programming, we are always trying to find ways to reduce the amount of code we are writing because less code equals less mistakes and less work. Yes, we all love less work!

A rendered view of the page—this is what the code produces.

Nerd note

In web design and programming, we are always trying to find ways to reduce the amount of code we are writing because less code equals less mistakes and less work. Yes, we all love less work!

CSS properties

CSS properties can include things like font types, text color, font size, text alignment, margins, and so much more. I will be introducing more of these "properties" throughout the book.

To be clear, CSS properties are a predefined list of things that you can change about your HTML with CSS. The <body> tag has a "background-color" property, for example, which you can use CSS to change from, say, white to purple.

Applying CSS to multiple pages

So, we've learned about CSS classes and how to apply them to a single page, but there are many times when you will be applying your styles to multiple pages, and it's a hassle to have to copy and paste the CSS code into each page. Not only would you be cluttering up each page with duplicate CSS code, but you would also find yourself having to edit each of these pages if or when you want to make a style change.

The solution is to create your CSS classes in a separate file, and then link it to the page you want to apply the code to, like this:

```
<link href="myFirstStyleSheet.css"
rel="stylesheet" type="text/css">
```

The above line of code links the external style sheet called "myFirstStyleSheet.css" to the HTML document. You place this code in between the <head> and </head> tags of your web page.

To create an external style sheet (an external CSS file), all you need to do is create a simple text document (just as you would for an HTML file) and then change the file type from ".txt" to ".css."

Windows:

On Windows, you simply right-click (in the folder where you want to place your CSS file) and select New -> Text document. Change the extension and confirm that you want to do this (1). As mentioned earlier, the filename extension tells the computer what kind of file it is and allows the computer to determine how to handle the file when, for example, you try to open it.

If you change a file name extension, the file might become unusable. Are you sure you want to change it?

① Yes   No

Using a good code editor

I am showing you here how to create CSS files with the simple text editors built into both Windows and Mac, but as we've said, when you actually get into building websites professionally, you will likely use a proper code editor. I want to stress that what makes a CSS document a CSS document is the code you write—as with HTML, you don't need to use a special app to create CSS documents (in contrast with say an Excel document or a Photoshop file).

Mac:

On Mac, you need to launch TextEdit, create a new document, and select Format -> Make Plain Text (2). Then save the file with a .css extension—you could call your page "style.css" as I have done here (3). A pop-up box will ask if you want to change the file extension; click the blue "Use .css" button.

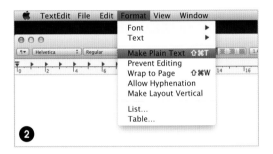

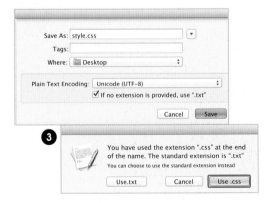

As you probably guessed, CSS files are just specially formatted text files, in much the same way as HTML pages are. There is nothing special or different about the file itself—rather it is the contents of the file that makes it a CSS document.

Note that when working with an external CSS document you don't need to add the tags below to the CSS file itself, in the way that you would if you embedded the CSS code in your HTML page:

```
<style type="text/css"></style>
```

Again, to be clear, you don't add the above code to your CSS stylesheets.

CSS learning tip

As I mentioned before, CSS is one of the hardest things to learn in web design—even programmers can have a hard time with it! So if you get frustrated at times, just keep this is mind and retry the simple examples in different ways. For example, create more classes, create another external style sheet and link to it, and so on.

When you link a CSS file to HTML web pages, the web browser is smart enough to know that you are linking to a CSS page. You don't need to declare (in the CSS page itself) that the code in the page is CSS. Instead you just add your CSS code directly to the style sheet like so:

```
.myNewStyle {
font-family: Verdana, Arial,
Helvetica, sans-serif;
font-weight: bold;
color: #FF0000;
}
.my2ndNewStyle {
font-family: Verdana, Arial,
Helvetica, sans-serif;
font-weight: bold;
color: #FF0000;
}
.my3rdNewStyle {
font-family: Verdana, Arial,
Helvetica, sans-serif;
font-weight: bold;
font-size: 12px;
color: #FF0000;
```

In the previous example I have created a series of CSS classes that can be applied to any HTML tag like so:

```
<p class="myNewStyle">My CSS styled
text</p>
```

Nerd terms for CSS

Style sheets and external style sheets are different ways of referring to the same thing—a separate page with CSS code in it.

or perhaps...

```
<h2 class="my3rdNewStyle">My CSS
styled text</h2>
```

You will notice that in the above example we applied a CSS style to an <h2> tag. All HTML tags have a default setting (if you will) with which it displays itself on the screen. The <h2> tag, by default, sets the text size to 24px (px = pixels). When we apply our CSS class to it, the CSS code overrides the default size that you would normally get with an <h2> tag, in favor of the size specified in the CSS class. So now you can see that CSS can override default HTML tag behavior!

CSS units of measurement

CSS has several size types that you can use to specify text size, among other things. The most commonly used are pixels and ems.

Unit	Description
%	percentage
in	inch
cm	centimeter
mm	millimeter
em	1em is equivalent to the height in pixels of the capital letter M in the current font size
pt	point (1pt is equivalent to 1/72 inch)
pc	pica (1pc is the same as 12 points)
pz	pixels (a dot on the computer screen)

CSS tag selectors

In the above examples we used CSS code that was written in the form of CSS classes; we then applied these CSS classes to various elements (tags) in the page. Another way to apply CSS is to globally redefine an HTML tag to look a certain way:

```
h1 { font-family: Garamond, "Times
New Roman", serif; font-size: 200%;
}
```

What this CSS code does is set the font style and size of all <h1> tags in one shot. Now you don't have to apply a CSS class to any <h1> tag, as they are all affected automatically by the CSS rules. This is an example of a CSS "tag selector." Here is another example, in which I give the whole page bigger margins:

```
body { margin-left: 15%; margin-
right: 15%; }
```

As you can see, you can redefine any tag and change the way it looks! This can be very powerful:

```
div { background: rgb(0,128,0);
padding: 0.5em;
border: 1px solid #000000;
}
```

Set in the previous code, any <div></div> tag will now have a background color of "rgb(0,128,0)" and have a padding of 0.5em and a thin one-pixel border that is solid black.

Expressing color with CSS

There are several things to explain about the example you have just seen. Color in CSS can be expressed in a few ways:

- In "hex," where #000000 is black and #FF0000 is red, for example.

- In "RGB," where rgb(255,0,0) would create red. (RGB is the acronym for "Red Green Blue.")

- With named colors, such as "Black" or "Red."

So the example on page 53 could alternatively be written like so:

```
div {
background: green;
padding: 0.5em;
border: 1px solid #000000;
}
```

Instead of "rgb(0,128,0)" I just specified "green."

Personally, I typically use hex colors, as I am familiar with them, or I just use named colors. By using RGB or hex color you have a lot more choice and can get the exact color you want more easily.

Hex colors

Hexadecimal color values start with the "#" symbol, and then have two digits for each primary color: red, green, and blue. The following hexadecimal color value creates a lime green color:

```
#32CD32
```

The first two digits represent the red component, the second two represent green, and the final two represent blue part of this color. It's similar to a painter's mixing palette.

Hex colors can be expressed in the six digit long form or a three digit short form. For example, both these codes create orange:

```
#ff6600
#f60
```

How to find color codes and names

Many programs (such as Adobe Dreamweaver) provide easy-to-use color pickers for you—this way, you don't need to remember the color codes by heart! Alternatively, you can find a list of the color codes at http://www.w3schools.com/cssref/css_colornames.asp (or simply do a search for "CSS color names").

The ColorZilla plugin for Firefox is another really useful way of finding color codes. You can either use the "eyedropper" tool within the browser window to identify a color shown on a website, or access a colour picker that gives you the codes for any color you choose.

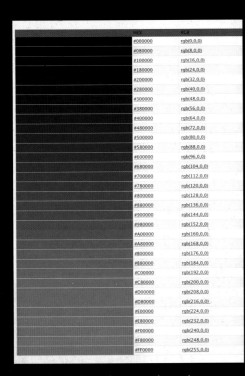

HEX	RGB
#000000	rgb(0,0,0)
#080000	rgb(8,0,0)
#100000	rgb(16,0,0)
#180000	rgb(24,0,0)
#200000	rgb(32,0,0)
#280000	rgb(40,0,0)
#300000	rgb(48,0,0)
#380000	rgb(56,0,0)
#400000	rgb(64,0,0)
#480000	rgb(72,0,0)
#500000	rgb(80,0,0)
#580000	rgb(88,0,0)
#600000	rgb(96,0,0)
#680000	rgb(104,0,0)
#700000	rgb(112,0,0)
#780000	rgb(120,0,0)
#800000	rgb(128,0,0)
#880000	rgb(136,0,0)
#900000	rgb(144,0,0)
#980000	rgb(152,0,0)
#A00000	rgb(160,0,0)
#A80000	rgb(168,0,0)
#B00000	rgb(176,0,0)
#B80000	rgb(184,0,0)
#C00000	rgb(192,0,0)
#C80000	rgb(200,0,0)
#D00000	rgb(208,0,0)
#D80000	rgb(216,0,0)
#E00000	rgb(224,0,0)
#E80000	rgb(232,0,0)
#F00000	rgb(240,0,0)
#F80000	rgb(248,0,0)
#FF0000	rgb(255,0,0)

The W3C website's color palette page, showing colors from dark to light red.

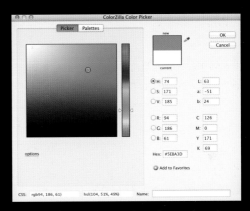

The free ColorZilla Firefox plugin has a built-in color picker you can use to select your colors.

Once installed, you can easily access ColorZilla in your browser top toolbar.

Applying mini CSS special effects

Let's have some fun! We are going to finish off this chapter with a few mini special effects that you can easily achieve with CSS. Let me emphasize that these are mini special effects, so don't expect to see Avatar 2 here!

Specifically, we are going to use something in CSS called "Pseudo-class selectors." Yep, this is a big nerd term but don't worry, we will get into this in the next chapter.

CSS roll-over links

In this example, we are going to use something called the "anchor pseudo-class." This is some specialized CSS that allows you to create link roll-over effects:

```
a:link { color: rgb(102, 102, 102)
}
a:visited { color: rgb(102, 0, 204)
}
a:hover { color: rgb(0, 96, 255)
}
a:active { color: rgb(255, 0, 102)
}
```

The above CSS will cause your link to change color when someone hovers their mouse pointer over it—instant rollovers with no fuss!

To explain things a little, the pseudo-class code in the previous example is:

:link (for unvisited links)
:visited (for visited links)
:hover (when mouse is over link)
:active (when link is clicked)

The "a" that appears before the pseudo-class code is the hyperlink tag, as in:

```
<a href="http://www.google.
com">Visit Google.</a>
```

One important note about the above code is that it is important to keep the style declarations are in the right order—link, visited, hover, active—otherwise it may not work in some browsers. My trick to easily remember the right declaration order is to just remember: LoVe-HAte.

Nerd note

"Anchors" are basically links, using HTML parlance.

```
<!DOCTYPE html>

<html>

<head>
<style>
a:link { color: rgb(102, 102, 102) } /* for unvisited links */
a:visited { color: rgb(102, 0, 204) } /* for visited links */
a:hover { color: rgb(0, 96, 255) } /* when mouse is over link */
a:active { color: rgb(255, 0, 102) } /* when link is clicked */
</style>

</head>

<body>
<h1>Welcome to My Homepage</h1>
<p>My name is Stef.</p>
<p>I live in Montreal.</p>
<p>My best <a href="http://www.webmentor.org">friend was Red</a> ... but she's
dead.</p>
```

The CSS rollover code highlighted in this screenshot.

Welcome to My Homepage

My name is Stef.

I live in Montreal.

My best friend was Red ... but she's dead.

The CSS rollover code in action. Yes, it's basic, but we've only just begun.

Styling the first line of a paragraph with CSS

Since we are on the subject of color and CSS, let's take a look at a CSS capability that's been made available more recently—the ability to target the first line of a paragraph. Here's the code:

```
p::first-line

{

background-color:#66cc66;

}
```

CSS and Color!

Lorem ipsum dolor sit amet, consectetur adipiscing elit. Aenean quis sapien pellentesque, egestas risus a, vehicula urna. Nam placerat ipsum non felis placerat, commodo posuere enim tempus. Mauris sem ipsum, blandit at aliquet eu, tincidunt non orci. Sed volutpat, dui vitae feugiat hendrerit, enim ligula auctor orci, et auctor purus sapien eget tellus. Praesent feugiat libero quis fermentum scelerisque. Donec eget neque vel justo luctus tempor a sit amet lectus. Fusce ut bibendum odio, sit amet bibendum dolor. Nulla sagittis orci a malesuada suscipit. Ut purus turpis, tincidunt in rutrum eu, laoreet sed lorem. Nam vitae lectus id augue congue varius. Phasellus aliquet leo id ultrices lacinia.

Colored first line code in action.

Welcome to My Homepage

Lorem ipsum dolor sit amet, consectetur adipiscing elit.

Aenean quis sapien pellentesque, egestas risus a, vehicula urna.

Nam placerat ipsum non felis placerat, commodo posuere enim tempus.

Our web page with ::first-letter applied. (I'm using Latin dummy text in this example. This is commonly used in the design world.)

Styling the first letter in a paragraph with CSS

This time, you are using CSS to target the first letter of every paragraph on the page. Here's the code:

```
p::first-letter {
color: red;
font-size: 200%;
}
```

The CSS ::after selector

This is one of my favorite selectors; it allows you to insert content (text or images) after whatever tag you want. In this case, I am inserting some text after each paragraph. For added pop, I am adding some "style" to the text:

```
p::after {
content: " - Famous quote by the
Roman poet Juvenal";
background-color: yellow;
color: gray;
font-weight: bold;
}
```

The nerds who created CSS, seemingly always wanting to keep things logical and balanced, created the opposite of the ::after selector—the ::before selector:

```
p::before {
content: "Important: ";
}
```

Yep, this CSS pseudo selector will insert the text "Important" before each paragraph.

Lorem ipsum dolor sit amet, consectetur adipiscing elit. Duis nec diam nibh. In eu faucibus dolor. Cras pretium eget diam et commodo. Aenean facilisis enim nisl, vitae sagittis nisi ultrices vitae. Sed risus eros, accumsan eu magna in, feugiat dapibus massa. Sed vel mauris vel nisi posuere accumsan sed eget diam. In imperdiet pretium libero, et faucibus arcu venenatis quis. Aliquam nec erat eget nibh suscipit congue ac vel lectus. Nulla ac orci dapibus, tincidunt turpis in, eleifend sem. Maecenas sed hendrerit sem, eleifend vestibulum felis. Maecenas porta pellentesque turpis dignissim fermentum. Cras ultricies, erat at ultrices vulputate, velit metus egestas mi, sed aliquet magna nunc in metus. Nulla et eros condimentum, lobortis metus vel, fringilla sapien. Aliquam ultricies laoreet dolor, sed tincidunt eros ultrices a. - Famous quote by the Roman poet Juvenal

The CSS ::after selector in action.

Wrapping up our first look at CSS

I've just scratched the surface of CSS here—I could write another couple pages just on CSS pseudo-class selectors alone! The good news is that you don't have to learn every single thing about CSS to be a great web designer—you just need to learn the basic principles and techniques.

The funny thing is, as you learn more you will probably forget some details and have to come back to this book to remind yourself of what the exact code is.

That said, in real-world web design work, you will only be using a small part of CSS on a regular basis. It's good to know all your CSS styling options, but don't make the mistake of thinking that you have to use some CSS trick somewhere (just because it exists)—you don't and you shouldn't. Always try to keep your pages

and your CSS code as simple as possible. That's what separates the professionals from the pretenders.

As I mentioned at the start of this chapter, learning CSS can be challenging, especially when you compare it to HTML. But if you find you are having problems understanding things, try not to worry too much. As you continue through the book—and write more code—the principles of CSS will slowly sink in.

CHAPTER 4

CSS in Action

Now that you have the first few chapters under your belt, you will be taking the next step toward total nerd glory with a three-part lesson on creating a website using CSS and CSS positioning.

Learning CSS can be hard, so you might get frustrated at points—I've had major headaches trying to wrap my head around CSS concepts!

The best way to approach this is first, to be patient, and second, write code. Writing code has a sneaky way of making your brain understand things (even if it usually doesn't come until the next day).

CSS is not just used to style text. Among other things, it is used for positioning elements on a web page. In other words, you will use CSS to create the basic layout and visual structure of your web pages.

What is CSS positioning?

In the old days of web design (up until about 2002), people used to use HTML table tags to lay out their web pages—

there was really no other way. But at some point the web browser makers (under pressure from web designers around the world) updated their browsers so that we could use CSS for page layouts.

Web designers everywhere rejoiced when that happened, because using CSS for page layout is far superior to using HTML tables, mostly because CSS-based layouts are much more flexible.

When I talk about layout, I am talking about creating the columns, headers and footers in your pages. Basically, CSS is used to position things on your pages using CSS positioning properties.

As you will see in Part 2, HTML tables are constructed using a set of HTML tags and are used for displaying data, just as a spreadsheet does. However, they

HEADER

3 NAV
· HOME
· ABOUT
· SERVICES
· CONTACT

1 CONTENT

2 SIDEBAR

Most web designers will start by creating diagrams to better conceptualize the website.

can be twisted and mangled to create a "scaffold" (if you will) for an entire web page. That comes at a great cost, though, in the form of a lot of extra code and a lack of flexibility in your web pages. Consequently, this is something you should never do today.

That said, CSS positioning can be confusing. Fortunately, I will be teaching you how to circumvent most of the frustrating aspects of CSS positioning and page layout. I just wanted to warn

you that you are now entering the dark side of web design, descending into the murky, messy depths of CSS positioning. So don't worry if you are confused at times—this is pretty normal when learning CSS positioning (or, as some people refer to it, "CSSP").

CSS template layout: Lesson 1

Let's jump into creating page layouts. To keep it simple we will only building a simple simple bare-bones web page. Nonetheless, by the end of this chapter you will be able to create CSS-based web pages. With this foundation you will be able to explore CSS further, as we do in Part 2 of the book.

Tags used in this CSS-based layout

One thing you will learn in this chapter is that the real complexity in web design is in the CSS and not really in the HTML. So in this page that we are about to build we will only be using six "types" of HTML tag. In Chapter 11 (p.192–4) we'll get into the HTML5 tags that add more meaning to a web page and even help simplify the code.

1. **<h>** The heading tags—which range from <h1></h1> to <h6></h6>—are going to be used to mark all of the headings in your pages. The most important heading will be wrapped in an <h1> tag and the least important in an <h6> tag. Here's an example of a heading:

```
<h1>CSS Template Layout</h1>
```

Heading tags help the search engines figure out what a page is about.

As mentioned, all browsers have a default size for each <h> tag, which determines how it renders text placed between these tags. Many of these defaults can be unusable (especially <h1>) because they come out too big, so CSS can be used to make the text sizes more to your liking.

2. **<p>** The paragraph tag is used to mark parts of the page as paragraphs— simple enough. A paragraph tag is what is called a "block element." That means that it acts like a "block," where a space is automatically inserted before and after each <p> tag pair. You will see this working in the examples coming up.

3. **<ul>** and **<ol>** These are list tags, which will be used to create your menus. The <ul> tag is the "un-ordered" list tag that creates a list with bullets or other images or icons that do not specify or denote an order (hence "un-ordered").

The <ol> tag is the "ordered" list tag. It creates a list that marks the list items with numbers or letters, instead of bullets. Code examples will follow.

4. **<div>** and **</div>** Div tags allow you to demark a portion of your page so that you can do things to it. Another way of saying "demark a portion" could be "put into a container." Once a part of your web page is in this <div> container you can do all kinds of stuff to it, such as style it, animate it, make it visible or invisible, and so on. Using <div> tags is the next generation of formatting HTML pages, superior to using tables in many ways.

You will use <div> tags to create containers for various parts of your page. One will be used to "hold" our navigational menu, and another to "hold" the main page.

5. **<a>** The most important tag in HTML is the <a> tag. Sometimes called the "hyperlink tag" it makes text "hyper" so that when you click on it you can load another page.

6. **<img>** This is the "image tag," which allows you to link to images so that they show up in your pages. In HTML, images are not embedded into the actual page; instead the image tag

What is HTML encoding?

For an HTML web page to display correctly, a web browser must know what character set (character encoding) to use. So how do you do this? With this line of HTML placed in between the <head> tag:

```
<meta charset="UTF-8">
```

What's a character set? It is how computers display text on screen. There are numerous character sets that you could use, but all you really need to use is UTF-8.

(<img>) only points to where the image is and the browser will attempt to load that image when a surfer loads your HTML page.

That covers the HTML tags you will use in your layout. As you know, there are many more tags you could use, but to keep things simple I suggest limiting yourself to these six (for now).

Creating the basic page template

To work through the examples, you are going to need a practice HTML page. To create your practice page, go to your desktop and create a simple text document. Name the file "chapter-4-1.html." Windows and Mac will show you a warning asking you if you want to change the file extension; just say "yes."

Open the file and type (or paste) the template code below. Remember that you can download the source files from the accompanying website, which will save you typing every little bit out.

```
<!DOCTYPE html>
<html>
<head>
<title>Chapter 4 CSS Tutorial
- No CSS Applied</title>
<meta charset="UTF-8">
</head>
<body>
</body>
</html>
```

This code forms the basic structure for all HTML pages. You can now add the code samples in between these tags:

```
<body><!--Insert code here! -->
</body>
```

One last note: between <body> and </body> in the previous code, you will find what is called a "comment."

Comments are a way to place notes that cannot be seen in the browser. Anything between the characters <!-- and --> becomes an HTML comment that is invisible in the browser.

So, in the above example, the word "and" would be invisible in the browser, meaning that it will not be displayed to someone viewing your web page. This is a good way to leave messages about what you are doing in the page. It can come in handy later on when someone else is working on the page or even when you are, because you may (you will!) forget why you did things a certain way.

Building the CSS

Once you have created the template page, create a folder and name it something like "my-website," and then drop the HTML page into it. In that same folder create a new text document and call it "chapter-4-css.css."

Open that file, add the following code, and then save it. Again, you can copy and paste the code from the source files—you don't need to type it all out.

Code comments

Both HTML and CSS have a way for you to leave text comments or messages behind that the browser ignores and does not display.

In HTML, comments look like this: <!-- this is a comment —>

In CSS, comments look like this: /* CSS comment */ (basically /* and */ with the comment in between).

```
/*** Tag Selectors ***/
body { font-family: Georgia, "Times
New Roman", Times, serif;
font-size: 14px; color: #333333;
background-color: #FFF;
}
p { width: 80%;}
ul li {
list-style-type: circle;
line-height: 200%;
ol li { list-style-type: numbers;
line-height: 180%;
width: 65%;
}
h1 { font-family: Georgia, "Times
New Roman", Times, serif;
font-size: 18px; font-weight: bold;
color: #000000;
}
h2 { font-family: Georgia, "Times
New Roman", Times, serif;
font-size: 16px; font-weight: bold;
color: #000000;
text-align: center;
}
h3 { font-family: Georgia, "Times
New Roman", Times, serif;
font-size: 14px; font-weight: bold;
color: #000000;
text-align: left; margin-top: 30px;
}
```

```
/*** Pseudo class Selectors ***/
a:link {color: gray; text-
decoration: none;}
a:visited { color: gray;
background: red; }
a:hover { color: blue; text-
decoration: underline;}
a:active { color: gray; font-
weight: bold;}
#centerDoc a:link {color: gray;
text-decoration: underline;}
#centerDoc a:hover { color: blue;}
/*** ID Selectors ***/
#navigation {position: absolute;
z-index: 10; width: 210px;
height: 600px; margin: 0; border-
right: 1px solid #000000;
font-weight: normal;
}
#centerDoc { position: absolute;
z-index: 15;
padding: 0 0 20px 20px; /*top right
bottom left*/
margin-top: 50px; margin-left:
235px; width: 80%;
}
#miamiBuilding { float: right;
margin: 10px; margin-bottom: 50px;
margin-right:20%
}
```

Don't let the CSS freak you out—I will soon explain the important details and you will see that there is nothing really complicated here.

There is one last thing to do before you finish this part of the tutorial—you need to add some code to your HTML page. Insert the following code between the <body></body> tags:

```
<div id="centerDoc">
<img id="miamiBuilding" src="miami.
png" height="350" width="193">
<h1>The Main Heading</h1>
<p>
Studioweb is an interactive video
question and answer training
system. We focus on teaching the
key basic concepts and techniques
of web design and web programming.
</p>
<h3>A Sub Heading</h3>
<p>
Studioweb is an interactive video
question and answer training
system. We focus on teaching the
key basic concepts and techniques
of web design and web programming.
Learn more:
</p>
<ol>
```

```
<li>Easily track student progress
through an easy to read
spreadsheet-like layout. Quickly
look over your classes to see where
students are in the courses. </li>
<li>View student profiles to get a
detailed view of your student's
progress: see scores and the badges
the student has earned.</li>
```

```
<li>Receive a verifiable "Certificate
of Completion" with each course you
finish. <a href="http://www.
studioweb.com" title="Web
Tutor">LEARN MORE!</a></li>
</ol>
<h3>Another Sub Heading</h3>
<p>
And so we have yet another
```

The Main Heading

Studioweb is an interactive video question and answer training system. We focus on teaching the key basic concepts and techniques of web design and web programming.

A Sub Heading

Studioweb is an interactive video question and answer training system. We focus on teaching the key basic concepts and techniques of web design and web programming..Learn more

1. Easily track student progress through an easy to read spreadsheet-like layout. Quickly look over your classes to see where students are in the courses.
2. View student profiles to get a detailed view of your student's progress: see scores and the badges the student has earned.
3. Receive a verifiable "Certificate of Completion" with each course you finish. LEARN MORE!

Another Sub Heading

And so we have yet another paragraph of text that follows our ordered list. The list is called an ordered list because it has an order imposed upon it by the web browser - the list of items are numbered.

The Main Navigation

- Home
- Store
- Blog
- Contact us

Your web page, not yet styled with CSS.

paragraph of text that follows our ordered list. The list is called an ordered list because it has an order imposed upon it by the web browser—the list of items are numbered.

```
</p>
</div> <!-- End of centerDoc div
-->
<div id="navigation">
<h2>The Main Navigation</h2>
<ul>
<li><a href=#>Home</a></li>
<li><a href=#>Store</a></li>
<li><a href=#>Blog</a></li>
<li><a href=#>Contact us</a></li>
</ul>
</div>
```

Now you have your HTML page and your CSS page, but they are not connected (linked). Before you link the two together, take a look at what the HTML pages look like before the CSS is applied—see the screenshot (1) on the previous page. Note how the image and the text appear on the HTML page—it's not too exciting, so let's apply the CSS.

To link the CSS to the HTML page, add the following HTML code in between the <head> </head> tags:

```
<link href="chapter-4-css.css"
rel="stylesheet" type="text/css">
```

All together, it should look like this in the <head> section:

```
<head>
<title>Chapter 4 CSS Tutorial—CSS
Applied!</title>
<meta charset="UTF-8">
<link href="chapter-4-css.css"
rel="stylesheet">
</head>
```

Once you've linked the CSS to the HTML page, the full effect of the CSS code will magically transform the HTML, as shown opposite (2). If you haven't set the page up yet on your own computer, please do so to make sure you have everything working so far.

Nerd note

Like most things in life, to really understand HTML and CSS, you must experience it. That means you have to write actual code and watch it not work, then—after pulling out some hair—you will figure it out! Eventually, you will develop your "nerd eyes" and all will be well.

The Main Navigation

- Home
- Store
- Blog
- Contact us

The Main Heading

Studioweb is an interactive video question and answer training system. We focus on teaching the key basic concepts and techniques of web design and web programming.

A Sub Heading

Studioweb is an interactive video question and answer training system. We focus on teaching the key basic concepts and techniques of web design and web programming. Learn more:

1. Easily track student progress through an easy to read spreadsheet-like layout. Quickly look over your classes to see where students are in the courses.
2. View student profiles to get a detailed view of your student's progress: see scores and the badges the student has earned.
3. Receive a verifiable "Certificate of Completion" with each course you finish. LEARN MORE!

Another Sub Heading

And so we have yet another paragraph of text that follows our ordered list. The list is called an ordered list because it has an order imposed upon it by the web browser—the list of items are numbered.

The page with the CSS applied.
Notice the shifted position of the menu.

CSS template layout: Lesson 2

In Lesson 1 you created a classic two-column layout with left side navigation using a little CSS and only a small number of HTML tags. The lesson presented the code for the page and explained which HTML tags you were going to use. Now let's take a closer look at the actual HTML code and CSS to see how it works.

Your page is really very simple. As you know, all the content (text, images, video, and so on) that the user sees when viewing a web page is marked-up with HTML in between the <body> and </body> tags. In this case, you have:

```
<!DOCTYPE html>
<body>
<div id="centerDoc">
<!-- I left out the details to save
space. We must save the trees! -->
</div>
<div id="navigation">
<!-- I left out the details to save
space. We must save the trees! -->
</div>
</body>
```

Breaking down the page template

Our page has two main sections, each enclosed inside <div> tags. As you learned in Lesson 1, <div> tags are designed to be used to create a division, or "container," in the document. You have created two such containers and given each of them a unique ID:

```
<div id="§">
<div id="navigation">
```

You will notice that the entire content of the page is contained in one of these two major page divisions. So the first questions are: what are the rules of IDs in HTML pages, and why do we use them and assign them to page elements like <div> tags?

First of all, you can assign IDs to any HTML tag, so you could assign an ID to a <p> tag as well.

An ID in a page should only be used once. That is to say that no two elements on any one page should have the same ID. This is because IDs are meant to uniquely identify a page element. In the previous example there is only one page element with an ID of "navigation," and only one page element with an ID of "centerDoc." I like to use ID names that talk to you—it is pretty clear what is going on in each division we created above.

IDs on HTML tags are used also used in CSS. We can target IDs in our CSS code to change the appearance, position, and even behaviour of that element by referencing the ID of the element.

Inside the <div> tags you use header tags (<h1> and <h2>) to set the headers. (I explained how header tags work in Lesson 1 of this tutorial.)

And finally we have <p> tags to hold the text that makes up this simple web page.

Attaching the CSS file

Now I am going to jump to the CSS file that is attached to the HTML page. You attach the CSS document using this line of code between the <head> </head> tags:

```
<head>
<link href="chapter-4-css.css"
rel="stylesheet">
</head>
```

Like the <a> tag, we have an "href" attribute—but this time pointing to the CSS document that has all our CSS code.

Let's break down the CSS link. First we specify the CSS file in the href attribute:

```
href="chapter-4-css.css"
```

... and then we tell the browser that the link is to a CSS style sheet with this attribute:

type="text/css."

All that is important in this example is that the link points to your CSS:

```
"chapter-4-css.css."
```

Breaking down the CSS file

Now that you have the style sheet linked to the HTML page, let's look at some CSS code. This first snippet of code "styles" the unique HTML IDs discussed previously:

```
#navigation {
position: absolute;
z-index: 10;
width: 210px;
height: 600px;
margin: 0px;
margin-top: 0px;
border-right: 1px solid #000000;
font-weight: normal;
}
#centerDoc {
position: absolute;
z-index: 15;
padding: 0 0 20px 20px; /*top right
bottom left*/
margin-top: 50px;
margin-left: 235px;
width: 80%;
}
```

There is a lot going on here, so let's focus on just a few elements for now. In this chunk of code there are two selectors ("#navigation" and "#centerDoc"), one for each ID. Each selector is followed by curly brackets: { }. In between the curly brackets is a list of the "properties" that specify what style to apply to the selector. Here is the CSS selector code with its properties removed:

```
#centerDoc {
        /*Look ma no CSS rules!*/
}
#navigation {
        /*Look ma no CSS rules!*/
}
```

To make things more clear, I removed the CSS code and just inserted the CSS comments: '/*Look ma no CSS rules!*/' to show you where the CSS code would normally be.

Hopefully you can see how we group CSS rules (inside selectors) using the curly brackets. Anything in between the curly brackets is part of one group or package that in CSS is generically called a property.

Selectors

With CSS, the selector's job is to select HTML tags on the page. There are many selectors in CSS, the most common being "id", "class," and "tag." Here is a quick example of using a tag selector in CSS—in this example "p" is the selector and it selects all the <p> tags in the page:

```
p {text-align: left; color:
purple;}
```

In our code, you can see that there is some text that appears before the curly brackets:

```
#centerDoc {}
#navigation {}
```

This text is the selector name. So our selectors are "centerDoc" and "navigation."

So why do we have the # symbol in front of the text? Why can't we call it simply "centerDoc" and "navigation?"

Understanding CSS selectors

As with HTML (and all programming languages), CSS uses certain symbols or text with a special meaning that tells the web browser something specific.

In this example, we are using the # symbol and that tells the web browser that we are targeting an HTML ID.

If you haven't fallen asleep yet, we can summarize by saying that we create a CSS ID selector for each HTML ID we have in our page.

Therefore, the CSS ID selector named "#centerDoc" applies to the <div>: <div id="centerDoc">. If you are having problems understanding now, just move on and write out the code—it will come.

What's an HTML "element?"

In a nutshell, a web page is made up of HTML elements. An HTML element is everything from the start of a tag to the end of the tag, including the content, as shown in the diagram below.

<h2>My Title</h2> ————— THIS IS AN HTML ELEMENT

<p>Like HTML (and ALL programming languages), text in certain places has a special meaning that tells the system (or the computer) to do something specific. In this case, whenever you have a "#" symbol in front of the name of a CSS selector, we are saying that this selector is a special type of selector called an "ID" selector. </p>

THIS IS ANOTHER HTML ELEMENT

If you wanted to get into detail, you can break down an HTML element into three sections:

• Start tag
• Element content
• End tag

These details come in handy as you get into more advanced page design, especially when you start using page animation and other special effects.

The CSS rules or styles you choose to add to your ID selector will change what appears inside the corresponding <div>. So, for the <div> with the ID of "navigation," you have these CSS rules:

```
#navigation {
position: absolute;
z-index: 10;
width: 210px;
height: 600px;
margin: 0;
margin-top: 0px;
border-right: 1px solid #C6EC8C;
font-weight: normal;
}
```

Notice at the bottom that it says all text will have a font-weight of "normal," by giving it this property:

```
font-weight: normal;
```

You could just as easily say that you want all the text to appear in the "navigation" <div> as bold instead, in which case the property would look like this:

```
font-weight: bold;
```

OK, let's get back to creating our page template. For this layout, we create the two column look with the CSS in the navigation and centerDoc <div>s.

First, the navigation <div> is sitting on the left and it has a border. How? The one-pixel border is created with this CSS:

```
border-right: 1px solid #C6EC8C;
```

Pretty self explanatory, no? I would suggest (as an exercise) changing the color of the border and changing the pixel thickness to see how it looks.

Alright, let's jump to the next thing: why is the navigation sitting on the left of the page, while the centerDoc is to the right? The first thing to look at is this line in the navigation selector:

```
position: absolute;
```

This tells the browser to just place this <div> on the page as is. This is perhaps oversimplifying the subject, but for our purposes this works for now.

The key to the two column look is in this CSS code:

```css
#centerDoc {
position: absolute;
z-index: 15;
padding: 0 0 20px 20px;
/*top right bottom left*/
margin-top: 50px;
margin-left: 235px;
width: 80%;
}
```

The line margin-left: 235px; tells the browser to insert 235px (pixels) of margin at the left of the centerDoc <div>. That pushes the centerDoc <div> over, thus allowing the navigation <div> to take that place (or, in this case, just create a column at the left).

However, before determining the margins, you need to set the "padding." Padding is space that wraps around our content.

Making CSS more compact

CSS code can be written in a compact way and in a long-form style. For example, consider this line of code:

```css
padding: 0 0 20px 20px;
/*top right bottom left*/
```

The CSS comments (/*top right bottom left*/) give you a clue about what's going on, but let's go a little deeper.

Padding can be set at the top, right, bottom, and left of a tag, so you could have: padding-top: 20px and padding-right: 15px.

The above code expresses the padding the compact way, where web browsers know that if you list four numbers in a row (as in padding: 0 0 20px 20px;) the first number represents the padding at the top, the second number represents the right side, the third number is the bottom, and the fourth is the left side.

That one line of code could also be written in the long-form style:

```css
padding-top: 0px;
padding-right: 0px;
padding-bottom: 20px;
padding-left: 20px
```

Nerd note

In CSS, if the value you set to something is 0 (zero), you don't have to specify that it is pixels, or any other unit that CSS uses.

HTML/CSS BOX MODEL

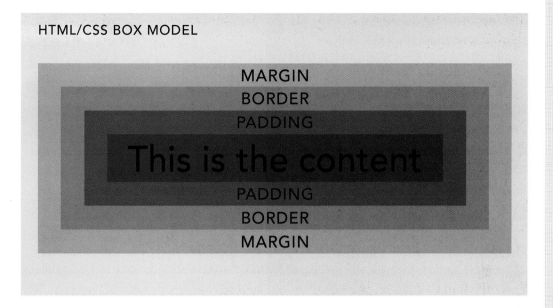

The CSS box model

CSS uses the concept of a box model that wraps around HTML elements. This box model consists of margin, border, padding, and the actual content (as shown above). This allows a border to be placed around elements and for elements to be spaced in relation to each other.

With our working example, anything between the <div> tags is the "content." After that comes the padding, then a border, and finally a margin.

Margin and padding may seem like the same thing, but being able to control the space before the border (the padding) and after the border (the margin) can really affect your layouts.

In the web page that you are currently working on, you will notice that the navigation <div> sits higher up on the page than the centerDoc <div>. This is not because of the order in which they appear in the HTML code. Rather, it is because of the margin settings given for each selector.

For the centerDoc <div>, the top margin is set to 50px:

```
margin-top: 50px;
```

For the navigation <div>, it is set to 0px:

```
margin-top: 0px;
```

Because the navigation <div> is set to 0 pixels, it is 50 pixels higher up than the centerDoc <div>. This is because the centerDoc <div> has a top margin of 50px, which pushes it down the page.

In the HTML, I would suggest moving the position of the #navigation <div> code, under the #centerDoc <div> code to see if it changes anything. You will see that the code's position does not change how things appear in the page because we use CSS positioning. It overrides what would normally happen.

Another thing to try is to play with the CSS values—change the padding, change the margins, etc. See what happens!

More about the CSS box model

The CSS box model (the virtual box we've been talking about) is key to CSS layouts. Typically, we use HTML <div> tags to create the page divisions, and then we manipulate the margin and padding size around them to position everything.

If you check out the screenshot at the right, you can see the box-model diagram at the bottom right, where the arrows indicate where the margins are on the web page—follow the red arrows in the image! In this case, there is 100px of margin at the left and right and no margin at the top and bottom.

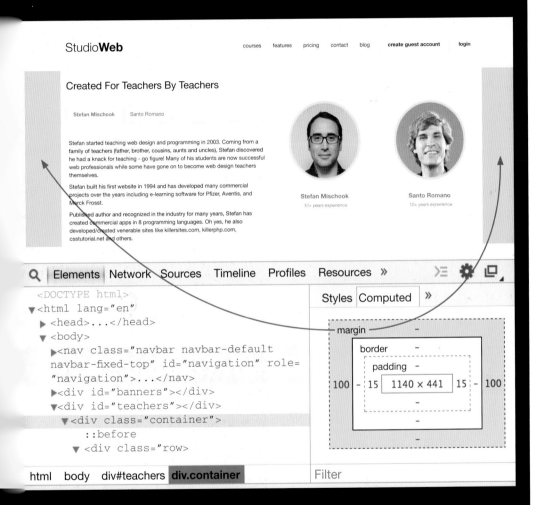

In this screen capture, I am using the Firefox web browser's built-in ability to inspect the code in a page—the tool is called "Inspect Element." As you can see, Firefox presents you with a live diagram of the box model of the div highlighted in the code: <div class="container">. I've added the red arrows to show how the diagram relates to the actual page—in this case, to the 100px margins at the left and right sides.

CSS template layout: Lesson 3

Lessons 1 and 2 were the hardest parts of building your template—everything gets really easy from here!

So far you've established your main document and the major sections are in place. All you need to do now is add your text and images.

Breaking down the page

This page is simple. We can start with a heading:

```
<h1>The Main Heading</h1>
```

And then a paragraph:

```
<p>
Studioweb is an interactive
video question and answer training
system. We focus on teaching the
key basic concepts and techniques
of web design and web programming.
</p>
```

We define how the paragraphs and the <h1> heading will look in the CSS code:

```
p { width: 80%; }
h1 {
font-family: Georgia, "Times New
Roman", Times, serif;
font-size: 18px;
font-weight: bold;
color: #000000;
}
```

This is pretty much self-explanatory. The only thing that should be mentioned is that you set the width of the <p> tags to 80%. This allows you to control the text width in one easy-to-edit spot.

Breaking down the navigation menu for our page

The last thing to talk about is the navigation menu. The best way to create a menu is by using list (<li>) tags. That makes sense, as navigational menus are essentially a list of pages.

The list item tags are styled with this CSS:

```
li {
list-style-type: circle;
line-height: 150%;
}
```

This code uses a circle for the bullet list items and makes the space between the listed items 1.5 times larger than normal (this is a personal choice; I like a little more "breathing room" between lines).

You have many options for list style types (called list item markers), including:

- circle
- square
- upper-roman
- disc
- lower-alpha

If you're feeling adventurous, try them all to see how they look—you can choose whichever one you like best.

Next, in the #navigation <div>, we have an unordered list (<ul>), just under the <h2> heading:

Using # as a placeholder

You may have noticed that I use the hash symbol (#) in the link's href attributes value, as in: <a href=#>Home</a>. Why? They are essentially just placeholders. When you put the # symbol in a link, nothing happens when you click on the link.

```
<h2>The Main Navigation</h2>
<ul>
<li><a href=#>Home</a></li>
<li><a href=#>Store</a></li>
<li><a href=#>Blog</a></li>
<li><a href=#>Contact us</a></li>
</ul>
```

Styling the other headings

You probably noticed in the HTML code that we have three heading types:

```
<h1>
<h2>
<h3>
```

And indeed, if you look at the CSS code listed on page 65, we did style all the headings, even though I did not get into details here. Why? Because we style all the headings with the same CSS—we just give different font size values to each header type.

The complete page in code (HTML)
as seen in my code editor.

```
OPEN FILES          chapter-4-2.html    x
 chapter-4-2.html
                1   <!DOCTYPE html>
                2   <html>
                3   <head>
                4   <title>Chapter 4 CSS Tutorial - CSS Applied!</title>
                5   <meta charset="UTF-8">
                6   <link href="chapter-4-css.css" rel="stylesheet">
                7   </head>
                8
                9   <body>
                10
                11  <div id="centerbox">
                12  <img id="miamiBuilding" src="miami.png" height="350" width="193">
                13
                14  <h1>The Main Heading</h1>
                15  <p>
                16  Studioweb is an interactive video question and answer training system. We focus on teaching the key basic concepts
                    and techniques of web design and web programming.
                17  </p>
                18
                19  <h3>A Sub Heading</h3>
                20  <p>
                21  Studioweb is an interactive video question and answer training system. We focus on teaching the key basic concepts
                    and techniques of web design and web programming. Learn more:
                22  </p>
                23
                24  <ol>
                25  <li>Easily track student progress through an easy to read spreadsheet-like layout. Quickly look over your classes
                    to see where students are in the courses. </li>
                26  <li>View student profiles to get a detailed view of your student's progress: see scores and the badges the student
                    has earned.</li>
                27  <li>Receive a verifiable "Certificate of Completion" with each course you finish. <a href="http://tutor.killersites.
                    com" title="Web Tutor">LEARN MORE!</a></li>
                28  </ol>
                29
                30  <h3>Another Sub Heading</h3>
                31  <p>
                32  And so we have yet another paragraph of text that follows our odered list. The list is called an ordered list
                    because it has an order imposed upon it by the web browser - the list of items are numbered.
                33  </p>
                34
                35  </div>
                36
                37  <div id="navigation">
                38  <h2>The Main navigation</h2>
                39  <ul>
                40  <li><a href="#">Home</a></li>
                41  <li><a href="#">Store</a></li>
                42  <li><a href="#">Blog</a></li>
                43  <li><a href="#">Contact us</a></li>
                44
                45  </ul>
                46  </div>
                47
                48  </body>
                49  </html>
```

Suggested exercises

A one page website is not exactly the most exciting thing! But when first learning, it's best to start simple—as we just did. But now that you've finished building your first page, it makes sense to practise by creating a few more.

If you check out the navigation, there are three more pages that you could build: store.html, blog.html, and contactUs.html. In the menu, we've used a placeholder symbol (#) instead of a web page address—when you create the other pages, you will have to replace the # with the page name. For example:

```
<a href="store.html">Store</a>
```

When you create the additional pages, be sure to link the external CSS file you created to them, to keep the style consistent across your site.

As an added exercise, try using some of the CSS pseudo selectors you learned about in the previous chapter, such as ::first-letter and ::first-line.

Wrapping up this chapter

That pretty much covers our goals for this chapter—good work! At the moment there isn't much content, but you could easily add to your pages, building them out to include lots of information, images, video, and other elements.

In Part 2 of the book, we will be covering much more advanced (and fun) CSS, so it's important that you understand the basics covered in Chapters 3 and 4.

Don't forget that when you run across things that are hard, it means you are training your brain in new ways. This is a good thing!

Formatting code

For this book, we've formatted (positioned) the code very tightly. However, when you write CSS for your own websites you are free to space out the CSS code in whatever way makes it easiest for you to read. In time, you will discover your own style of formatting your code.

CHAPTER 5

Digging Deeper into Web Design

Theory can be tough. Yet, there is no denying that there are times when you just have to bite down and eat your vegetables!

You can get up and running quickly with web design, as the basics are pretty easy to understand. However, to take full advantage of HTML and CSS you need to start digging into some of the advanced topics.

In this chapter, you are going to start delving deeper into HTML, before getting into CSS in the same way. This will help you understand the finer details of these languages, which will make your web design work much easier.

You will finish off the chapter learning about the three image types used in web design.

Modern websites make use of huge images. This is possible due to advanced CSS techniques and faster Internet speeds. Ref: http://watb.co.uk

HTML below the surface

More about doctypes

In Chapter 1 (when you were a web design greenhorn) I talked about browser engines and doctypes. Let's expand on that.

First, the doctypes I listed represented different versions of HTML—and there have been a few: HTML, HTML 2, HTML 3.2... all the way up to HTML5. There is no point in listing all the HTML versions because you don't to really need to know about any of them except for HTML5. Since the doctype tells the web browser which version of HTML to use, if you decided (for some crazy reason) to use the HTML 4.01 doctype, the web browser would process the page with that engine. You've been using the HTML5 doctype since the beginning of the book. Because of the way HTML5 works (and all later versions of HTML), you will never need to change the doctype. The HTML5 doctype is the final doctype version you will have to use!

What is XHTML?

XHTML is just some silly HTML-like language (it's actually a language called XML) that was king of web design for a few years until HTML5 won. It's different in some key ways, but I will not get into

Big images can make a website look great—ideally they should convey a message or meaning about the site. Ref: http://getden.co.uk

that here—and so the future is HTML5. I mention it because you may run into XHTML on occasion if you are working on some older sites, but don't be too worried about it: except for some nitty-gritty details, HTML5 and XHTML operate and look very much the same. How do you know if the page is using XHTML? The doctype will tell you:

```
<!DOCTYPE html PUBLIC "-//W3C//DTD
XHTML 1.0 Strict//EN" "http://www.
w3.org/TR/xhtml1/DTD/xhtml1-strict.
dtd">
```

This Polish site uses the HTML5 <video> tag to clever effect. (More about this in Part 2.)
Ref: http://hushselected.com

I'm not going to get into the details of XHTML because it is a technology that is disappearing fast (and I never liked it to begin with), but if you are a glutton for punishment, you can read all you want about XHTML here:

http://www.w3schools.com/html/html_xhtml.asp

While you're at it, given that you might like old tech, check this out:

http://en.wikipedia.org/wiki/Typewriter

What is semantic HTML?

Semantic HTML is HTML that tells you about the meaning of the web page, not just the placement of things. For example, the <p> tag tells you this is a paragraph of text. The semantic meaning of tags are designed to describe (to the browser) the enclosed elements' meaning. Other examples of semantic HTML tags include <h1> to <h6> header tags. As you know, these are what tell you the text in between is a header—like a newspaper headline. This implies that the text is more important than the text you would find in a paragraph. Header tags also tell you how important the header is: a header with an <h1> tag is considered more important that an <h2> tag, <h2> is more important than <h3>, and so on.

<div> tells you that this is a logical division from the other parts of a page.

<blockquote> tells you that the text is a quotation.

The list goes on, but why should you care about semantic HTML? There are several good reasons:

- **Easier page editing**: Semantic tags make editing and maintaining websites easier because of the meaning that the tags convey to web designers. For example, in HTML5 the following tags were specifically added to make it easier to add meaning to web pages:

  <header> tells you this is header.

  <footer> tells you this is a footer.

  <nav> tells you this is the navigation for the site.

  How does this help? Well, say you come back to edit a site several months after building it. Being able to immediately see the meaning of sections will make the process a whole lot easier. It will also help if someone else has to update your work. It's like leaving notes behind.

- **Accessibility**: One of the key goals in modern web design is to make websites easier for people to navigate with screen readers and other assistive tools. Semantic tags help a lot when it comes to this. Think about, say, the <h1> tag—this will tell screen readers that this is a header, and so it can convey this meaning to the visually impaired.

- **Search Engine Optimization**: Google and other search engines use programs called search bots that catalog the web. Semantic tags help these programs figure out what your pages are about. Having pages that are properly semantically structured can only help your search engine rankings. For example, going back to the <h1> tag, whatever text you have in it suggests to the Google bot that the page has a lot to do with that heading.

What about SEO?

SEO—short for Search Engine Optimization—is the practice of revamping code in a website so that it is more search engine bot friendly.

SEO used to be largely done by third party SEO experts. Today it is typically the job of web designers because if you build a website with modern methods, as taught in this book, your sites are already optimized. Second, the search engines are very sophisticated these days; they can figure things out about websites much more effectively than before.

```
    OPEN FILES
    default-browser-...        default-browser-tag-display.html  ×
    1  <!doctype html>
    2  <html lang="en-US">
    3  <head>
    4      <meta charset="utf-8">
    5      <title></title>
    6  </head>
    7  <body>
    8
    9  <h1>I love bananas.</h1>
   10
   11  <h2>I love cake.</h2>
   12
   13  <h3>I love custard pie.</h3>
   14
   15  <h4>I love donuts.</h4>
   16
   17  <h5>I love peanuts.</h5>
   18
   19  <blockquote>I only reason I mention this, is so that you don't get
       confused when you start building pages and you see the default
       styling of things appear on your page. This is something that I've
       seen confuse people in the past.</blockquote>
   20
   21
   22  </body>
   23  </html>
```

HTML code as it is displayed in the default way.

I love bananas.

I love cake.

I love custard pie.

I love donuts.

I love peanuts.

> I only reason I mention this, is so that you don't get confused when you start building pages and you see the default styling of things appear on your page. This is something that I've seen confuse people in the past.

How browsers display tags

Although CSS allows you to style your page elements (text, images, and so on), web browsers have a default way of displaying things.

Let's take the <h1> tag as an example. By default, browsers will make the text appear bold and increase the font size between the <h1> and </h1> tags. But it is understood that CSS will be used by web designers to give them a proper style. Nonetheless, all tags have a default look that browsers give them.

The reason I mention this is so you don't get confused when you start building pages and see the default styling appear on your page. This is something that I've seen confuse people in the past.

PS: You will notice in the screenshots above that I've included a <blockquote> to show you how its browser default looks (it indents the text).

Block-level tags vs. inline tags

On pages 75–77 you were introduced the CSS box model. I am going to look at that again, so you can get into more detail.

In HTML, there are two broad tag categories—tags can be either "inline" or "block level."

Block-level tags exist in their own virtual "box" and are always followed by a line break (like hitting the "Enter" key after typing in some text). In other words, a block-level tag breaks the flow of text and other elements to create a virtual box around itself. This virtual box is often called the "box model" (see the diagram on page 78).

Here is a short list of some of the block-level tags: <p>, <div>, <blockquote>, <table>, <form>, <ul>, and <ol>.

Inline tags (elements) become a part of the "flow" of text in which they are inserted; they have no virtual box around them and so they don't have the line break either. Examples of inline tags include: <strong>, <a>, <em>, <img>, and <span>.

Properly nesting tags

Let's finish our look at HTML (in this chapter) with proper tag nesting. Proper tag nesting is like being sure your bird's eggs are nicely settled in the bird's nest. You can't have your eggs hanging halfway outside of the nest—they might break!

So how does my stupid analogy translate into real-world HTML? Basically, you want to be sure that your tags don't get mixed up. Here is an example of proper tag nesting:

```
<p> Some text … and this is
some <strong> important text. </
strong> <p>
```

Now this is bad:

```
<p> Some text … and this is some
<strong> important text. </p> </
strong>
```

In the second example above, the <strong> tag opened inside the <p> tag, so you must be sure to close the <strong> tag inside the <p> tag as well (as in the first example). When you don't properly nest your tags like this, it can really screw up your pages. So nest them properly if you know what's good for you!

Under the hood of CSS

Let's step away from HTML for a little bit and give CSS some attention. As I mentioned in Chapters 3 and 4, you've only just begun to explore CSS, so let's not waste any more time!

Using CSS to change block level tags to inline tags

CSS gives you the power to change the default behavior of any tag. So, you can change a tag that is naturally a block-level tag into an inline tag using this CSS code:

```
p { display: inline; }
```

In the above example, this changes the paragraph tag so it acts like an inline tag. Let's transform an inline tag into a block-level tag.

```
<!DOCTYPE html>
<html>
<head><title>Inline tags to block-level using CSS</title>
</head>
<body>
<h2>Nerd details in code: </h2>
<p>Lorem ipsum dolor sit amet, consectetur adipiscing elit. Pellentesque ut diam porttitor justo convallis suscipit vestibulum non turpis. Aliquam vel lacinia tortor. Praesent interdum fermentum odio, sed molestie dui ornare in. Ut posuere dolor et lorem semper mollis. Maecenas vel tortor nulla. Cum sociis natoque penatibus et magnis dis parturient montes, nascetur ridiculus mus. Cras quis ex tristique, eleifend lectus nec, placerat neque. Morbi vehicula efficitur ligula id rutrum. Mauris pharetra dictum massa, a <span>... THIS IS THE TARGET TEXT .... </span>. Ut pharetra urna nec viverra maximus. Duis varius fringilla arcu, a efficitur lectus posuere sit amet. Fusce at porttitor neque, ut egestas lorem. Sed iaculis vel nunc a eleifend. Donec dignissim libero a erat posuere ultrices. Nam vitae faucibus dui. </p>
</body>
</html>
```

In the above example, notice that I inserted the <span> tag in the large paragraph of Latin text. As you know, the <span> tag is used to section off or isolate text so that you can then use CSS to easily style it.

Inline tags to block-level using CSS

Lorem ipsum dolor sit amet, consectetur adipiscing elit. Pellentesque ut diam porttitor justo convallis suscipit vestibulum non turpis. Aliquam vel lacinia tortor. Praesent interdum fermentum odio, sed molestie dui ornare in. Ut posuere dolor et lorem semper mollis. Maecenas vel tortor nulla. Cum sociis natoque penatibus et magnis dis parturient montes, nascetur ridiculus mus. Cras quis ex tristique, eleifend lectus nec, placerat neque. Morbi vehicula efficitur ligula id rutrum. Mauris pharetra dictum massa, a ... THIS IS THE TARGET TEXT .... Ut pharetra urna nec viverra maximus. Duis varius fringilla arcu, a efficitur lectus posuere sit amet. Fusce at porttitor neque, ut egestas lorem. Sed iaculis vel nunc a eleifend. Donec dignissim libero a erat posuere ultrices. Nam vitae faucibus dui. **1**

```
<!DOCTYPE html>
<html>
        <head><title>Inline tags to block-level using
CSS</title>
        </head>
        <body>
                <h2>Inline tags to block-level using CSS</h2>
                <p>Lorem ipsum dolor sit amet, consectetur
adipiscing elit. Pellentesque ut diam porttitor justo
convallis suscipit vestibulum non turpis. Aliquam vel lacinia
tortor. Praesent interdum fermentum odio, sed molestie dui
ornare in. Ut posuere dolor et lorem semper mollis. Maecenas
vel tortor nulla. Cum sociis natoque penatibus et magnis dis
parturient montes, nascetur ridiculus mus. Cras quis ex
tristique, eleifend lectus nec, placerat neque. Morbi
vehicula efficitur ligula id rutrum. Mauris pharetra dictum
massa, a <span style="display: block; color: gray">... THIS
IS THE TARGET TEXT ...</span>. Ut pharetra urna nec viverra
maximus. Duis varius fringilla arcu, a efficitur lectus
posuere sit amet. Fusce at porttitor neque, ut egestas lorem.
Sed iaculis vel nunc a eleifend. Donec dignissim libero
a erat posuere ultrices. Nam vitae faucibus dui. </p>
        </body>
</html>
```
2

For example, you might want to always make a certain set of words flash when someone mouses over it. The <span> tag is one way to wrap around these words and literally "tag" them. Check out how the paragraph looks when I've kept the <span> tag set to its default of being an inline tag (1).

Now look at this code (2), where I've added some CSS to change the <span> from inline to block-level. I have also made the font gray so it's more visible.

Finally, see how the page has been changed by the new code (3).

Inline tags to block-level using CSS

Lorem ipsum dolor sit amet, consectetur adipiscing elit. Pellentesque ut diam porttitor justo convallis suscipit vestibulum non turpis. Aliquam vel lacinia tortor. Praesent interdum fermentum odio, sed molestie dui ornare in. Ut posuere dolor et lorem semper mollis. Maecenas vel tortor nulla. Cum sociis natoque penatibus et magnis dis parturient montes, nascetur ridiculus mus. Cras quis ex tristique, eleifend lectus nec, placerat neque. Morbi vehicula efficitur ligula id rutrum. Mauris pharetra dictum massa, a
... THIS IS THE TARGET TEXT ....
Ut pharetra urna nec viverra maximus. Duis varius fringilla arcu, a efficitur lectus posuere sit amet. Fusce at porttitor neque, ut egestas lorem. Sed iaculis vel nunc a eleifend. Donec dignissim libero a erat posuere ultrices. Nam vitae faucibus dui. **3**

Grouping CSS selectors

You can save space by grouping your CSS selectors together—e.g., take these:

```
h3 {color: black;}
h4 {color: black;}
.cssClassOne { color: black;}
.cssClassTwo { color: black;}
```

Now group them:

```
h2, h4, .cssClassOne, .cssClassTwo
{ color: black;}
```

Immediately, three lines of code have become one. The key is to have a comma (,) between each CSS selector.

Descendant selectors

CSS has all kinds of selectors that you can use to "select" HTML in your pages, which makes for some fun styling opportunities. However, most of the time the different selector types are there to help minimize the code you need to write.

The descendant selector allows you to target tags only when they appear inside other tags. For instance, let's say you wanted to change the background color of a <p>, only if it was in a <div>. This is the code to use (note the space between the div and the p):

```
div p {
background-color: brown;
}
```

Don't mix this up with grouping—if you put a comma between the div and p you would have grouped the selectors, and this is not the same thing at all! CSS is very picky, so your code needs to be exact.

The inner mechanics of CSS

To really understand how CSS works on your pages you need to get into some pretty intricate stuff. So let's look at the logic (if you will) of how the CSS engine processes your CSS code. There are three basic things that have a global impact on how CSS works—they are:

1. CSS placement

2. CSS inheritance

3. CSS cascade and specificity.

Although you are going to get into some detail here, you are not going to go too far down this nerd rabbit hole. However, you will have more than enough insight to build good sites with confidence.

A word of caution, though: you may have to reread this part once or twice, sleep on it, and have a coffee before it begins to sink in. But believe me, you will be glad that you did, because it will save you from major headaches down the road when you are building websites and you can't figure out why a hyperlink is red, when you thought it was supposed to be green.

1. CSS placement

The order of placement of your CSS code (in your pages and website) determines which code operates on a piece of HTML in your pages. For example, let's say you have a CSS rule in the <head> of your page that sets the <h1> tag color to red:

```
<!doctype html>
<html lang="en-US">
<head>
<meta charset="utf-8">
<title>The Cascade in CSS</title>
<style>
h1 { color: red;}
</style>
</head>
<body>
```

However, in the confusion of writing your code, you actually placed some CSS inline, right on an <h1> tag as well.

Here's the code snippet:

```
<body>
<h1 style="color: blue;">This
is my header ...</h1>
</body>
```

The problem you have here is that you've set the color to <h1> in two different places on your page—and to two different colors! So which CSS rule will be used by the browser?

Basically, the CSS selector that is closest to the target element will be the one that has seniority. In this case, your <h1> will be blue. To summarize, this is the hierarchy of CSS placement:

1. Inline CSS: right on the tag always wins!

2. In-page CSS: not as powerful as inline CSS, but more dominant than 3.

3. External CSS: these pages of CSS code can be overridden by the previous two.

It makes sense that CSS placement works this way, because this gives you the flexibility of setting site-wide global styles, while still being able to apply specific CSS rules to particular pages using in-page CSS or (very rarely) inline CSS.

A final CSS placement rule is that web browsers process code from the top of the page and work their way down. So if you have this code:

```
<style>
h1 {color: black;}
h1 { color: red;}
</style>
```

The color will be red, as the <h1> that has the color set to red comes after the <h1> that sets it to black.

2. CSS inheritance

In a nutshell, CSS rules (for example: body {color: blue; font-size: 18px;}) will "flow" down the page like water cascading down a waterfall. (I'm pretty sure those responsible for inventing "Cascading Style Sheets" chose the name based on this idea.) So let's say you have this page (I'm just showing the code you need to see, to save some trees):

```
<head>
<style>
body {color: blue; font-size:
18px;}
</style>
</head>
<body>
```

```
<h1>This is my header …</h1>
<p>This is a paragraph of text. The
other day, I visited my grandma and
she baked me a rhubarb pie. </p>
</body>
```

As the color is set to blue for the <body>, any text in the <body> will be blue. That's all the text, including text in all the <p> tags, all the <h1> tags, and any other tags! Can you see how the CSS rule literally cascaded down the page? In other words, <p> inherited the blue text color from the <body>.

The Document Object Model (DOM)

Understanding how the DOM hierarchy effects which CSS rules get applied will save you a lot of time when chasing bugs.

The DOM is a virtual map of your webpage, which shows you the hierarchy of how the page is structured. Take a close look at the diagram above that details this hierarchy and notice how some tags are "children" of other tags, in that they fall inside their parent tag. In the diagram you can see that all the tags that come after the <body> tag are children of <body>. You can also see another child-parent relationship between the <ul> tag and its children, the three <li> tags.

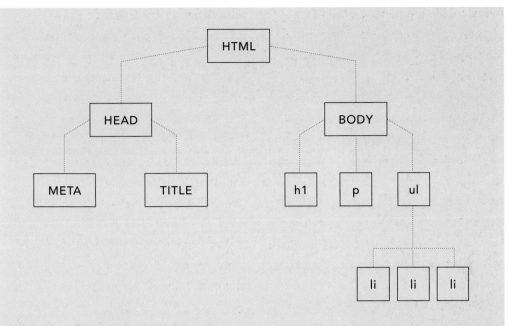

```
<html>
<dhead>
<meta http-equiv="Content-Type"
content-"text/html; charset-utf-8"/>
<title>     </title>
</head>

<body>
<h1>The Javascript DOM</h1>

<p>the DOM is short for Documant Object Model. But the M in DOM could
just as easily stand for Map because the DOM is just a MAP of the web
page that's currently loaded in the browser</p>
<ul>
<li>DOCUMENT = the web page</li>
<li>OBJECT = virual objects</li>
<li>MODEL + map</li>
</ul>
</body>
</html>
```

On the other hand, you can see that the <p> tag on the page—although it comes up before the <ul> tag in the code (underneath the diagram)—is not the parent of <ul> because <ul> doesn't reside inside <p>. In a nutshell, for a tag to be a child of another tag, it has to sit inside that parent tag.

On this page, the <p> tag, the <h1> tag, and the <ul> tag are just siblings. This takes us back to the cascading action in CSS: the cascade works downward in the hierarchy—parent to child, to grand-children, and to great grandchildren. In this example, if you set the text color in <p> to blue, this CSS rule would have

no impact on <ul>, as <ul> is not a child of <p>. However, if you set the text color to blue in <body>, the <ul> tag (and all other tags under <body>) would then be affected by this rule and all the text would be blue.

Hopefully you can see now that CSS inheritance has everything to do with the DOM. But how does CSS inheritance help? Well, with CSS inheritance you can simplify and reduce the amount of CSS code needed, which will make your sites easier to build and manage.

For example, if you want the text in your page to be black, you could target each tag in your page like an uneducated nerd:

```
p, h1, h2, h3, div, ul, ol, li
{color: black;}
```

Or you could be a little bit smarter about it and use inheritance:

```
body {color: black;}
```

The DOM helps iron out bugs

It's happened to me many times that I've had a CSS rule in my external style sheet (which 99% of your CSS should be in so you don't have a nightmare keeping things organized) that just wasn't working. When I checked the page that was having problems, I found some dirty CSS code in there that was overriding my external style sheet.

3. CSS cascade and specificity

In even modestly complex style sheets you can have rules that conflict. You've seen how placement can help to resolve that, but the cascade also helps to solve these conflicts with its rule of specificity.

Basically, a more specific tag selector overrides less specific tag selectors. Check out this simple example:

```
<style>
h1.firstHeading {color: black;}
h1 { color: red;}
</style>
</head>
<body>
<h1 class="firstHeading">This
is my header …</h1>
</body>
```

Here there is a class called "firstHeading," which has been applied to the first heading tag.

In the CSS, there's a rule for <h1> tags that has a firstHeading class applied to it:

```
h1.firstHeading {color: black;}
```

Right under it is a less specific CSS rule for all <h1> tags. Even though the second CSS rule (for all <h1> tags) comes after the specialized <h1> CSS rule, the first CSS rule is specialized, so it overrides the more generic CSS. This is despite the more generic <h1> CSS rule falling after it. So, while placement would usually favor the generic rule, this has been overridden by specificity.

Nerd note

ID selectors are more specific than class selectors. Just something to keep in mind!

Images in web design

Whoa! This is a big one—the use of images in web design is a hugely important subject! Images are a key component of most websites and they also play an important role in helping to set the tone of a site (along with page colors and fonts).

There's a lot to cover here, but hopefully it should be pretty easy to understand. Let's start with some general rules about images in websites:

• You don't want to have huge file sizes in web design, as people have to download them when they load your pages. File sizes are generally less important in today's age of YouTube and HD video streaming, but you should still be mindful of this. Where you should consider it most carefully is with mobile; not everyone has huge data plans, so if the mobile web surfer is important to you, you should be aware of that.

• When you save your images for websites, they only need to be sized at 72 pixels per inch (ppi). Images for print are typically 300ppi.

• Image preparation in modern web design is a much smaller part of the job than it used to be. In fact, many times you will be downloading pre-optimized images from photo banks or your clients will provide them—outputting at 72ppi isn't exactly brain surgery. Web designers prepping images in modern web design is akin to a carpenter cutting down his own trees. You may have to do it sometimes, but it is becoming a smaller and smaller part of the process.

The three image file types used in websites

You basically have three image types to choose from for your web pages:

1. JPEG (JPG) is best for photos with millions of colours.

2. PNG is best for flat colored images or images where you need complex transparency. (See over, page 101).

3. GIF is best for small icons and images with simple transparency needs.

Each image format ("format" is just a term for how the image is built in computer code) has its strengths and weaknesses, so the best choice will depend on the kind, and use, of the image.

This example shows the best use of PNG, JPEG, and GIF images in this web page.

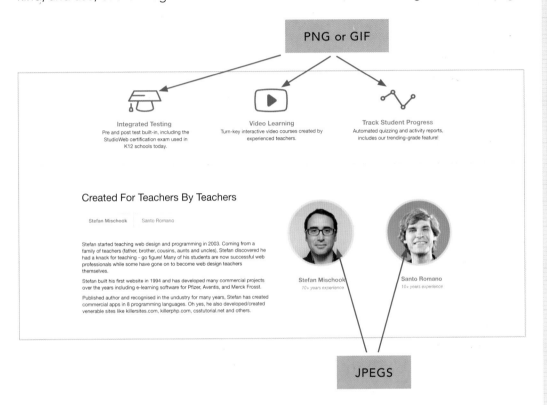

JPEGs

A JPEG is an HD image file type, which uses 24 bits to hold its image data and so it is used to create highly detailed images with millions of colors. JPEGs are best used when you want to include photographs in your web pages.

Beyond that, JPEGs do a very good job compressing images while still looking good. The more you compress a JPEG image, the smaller its file size becomes. However, you have to be careful that you don't compress JPEGs too heavily, as the compression process can degrade the image.

Every image-editing program out there (such as Photoshop or GIMP) can output images in JPEG format. It is universal. When you output an image to JPEG,

you will have a bunch of options to be able to tweak the quality of the image. There is a balance between keeping the JPEG size reasonable while keeping the image looking good. Use your eyes!

JPEG is a "lossy" file format, which means every time you save (and re-save) an image as a JPEG, information is lost in the process. If you keep re-saving your images over and over, the quality will keep dropping and you will eventually have a rotten-looking photo filled with jagged edges, blotches, and washed-out colors—these things are called "image artifacts" or "compression artifacts." This means it's a good idea to always keep your original image or photo so you can go back to it should you need to make a change.

PNG

PNG is another HD image format with 24 bits of information. It's a newer format than JPEG and is best used for images with solid colors, such as logos.

PNG can make photographs look great too, as PNG is a 24-bit format, but the PNG compression is not as efficient as JPEG, so the resulting file sizes are bigger. On the other hand, PNG compression is lossless, so you can re-save a PNG file over and over without any loss of quality.

Ideal compression for images

I've found over the years that the optimal output setting for JPEGs is about 80% compression—regardless of the photo editor you use. You seem to get a great image at this setting, while reducing the file size.

Transparency

The three rainbow-colored circles are outputs of the same image in JPEG, GIF, and PNG formats. The JPEG has no transparency, so you can see the dark background around the circle. The GIF has a simple transparency, so you get a clean circle floating over the white page. In this example, the PNG is the best, as it allows a nice gradual transparency, with the circle fading into the white page behind it.

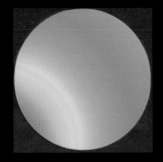

JPEG images do not support transparency.

GIF images have simple on/off tranparency.

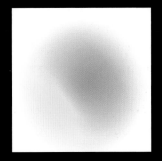

PNG images have graduated blended transparency.

PNG files also support 24-bit transparency (sometimes called an alpha channel) so PNG images can create some really cool effects in websites like, say, gradually fading images that overlay a background.

GIF

The GIF format is an 8-bit format that was created in 1987. It's main use is for small icons and images that require simple transparency. A simple transparency is one where a pixel in your image is either 100% transparent, or it is not. This limitation is due to the fact that a GIF is an 8-bit format, which means it can only display 256 colors, compared to the 16.7 million colors of a PNG or JPEG file. However, the 8-bit advantage is that it keeps your GIF file sizes really small. Simple animations are also possible with GIFs. There are many apps that will allow you to output simple GIF animations, including Adobe Fireworks, Adobe Photoshop, and Microsoft GIF Animator.

GIF cinemagraphs

A current trend in web design is the use of something called a "cinemagraph." This is basically a huge animated GIF that is used as the background of a web page. This is almost a "poor man's" full-screen video, although you can still get great-looking results without the load that true full-screen video burdens you with.

This chapter's done—what's next?

We've covered a lot in this chapter—we've jumped deep into the web design pool! So next, we are going to dive even deeper and learn the very basics of (gulp!) web programming with JavaScript!

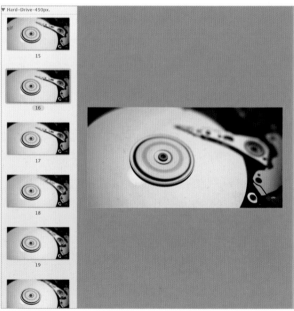

Free to use cinemagraphs.
Ref: http://www.freecinemagraphs.com

The websites pictured left are all examples of modern web design. You will find the use of fullscreen background video, large images and innovative yet intuitive menus.
Refs:
http://www.borngroup.com
http://www.tondapizza.it
http://www.iambaaz.com

CHAPTER 6

An Introduction to JavaScript

In modern web design you need to understand code. That's not just HTML and CSS—you've also got to go for the powerful stuff, which means learning a little bit about programming!

JavaScript is the programming language built into every web browser. JavaScript is there so that web designers can "talk" directly to web browsers, allowing you to do some pretty cool things. It is such an important part of modern web design that you just can't ignore it— especially if you want a job!

This chapter will introduce you to JavaScript and basic programming concepts. There's not the space to turn you into a programmer, but simply understanding these basic points will make your job as a web designer easier.

The goal for this chapter is to get you used to some of the concepts found in the JavaScript programming language.

These ideas are also found in many other popular programming languages, such as Java, Ruby, and PHP, among others (note that Java and JavaScript are NOT the same language). With a fundamental understanding, you will be able to more easily use the popular JavaScript libraries that web designers rely on almost daily. Besides that, if (and probably when) you decide to learn how to build web apps, it will be much easier for you.

I know it may seem unrelated now, but once you start catching on you will see how it is all connected. Soon, JavaScript, Ruby, PHP, and many other programming languages and technologies will become much more approachable.

Designers—don't be scared at this point! I started out as a graphic designer with no technical background, other than a basic understanding of HTML. Then in 1995, I made the decision to learn JavaScript, followed by several other languages. It was one of the best decisions I've ever made—and if I can do it, so can you!

Why should you learn programming in a web-design book?

First of all, you are only going to scratch the surface of programming. That said, there is a good reason to include the basics of programming in a web design book. Modern day web design is much more about code, structure, and a whole bunch of other things that go way beyond making the pages look pretty.

There are many things that web designers have to do daily, and this is where basic programming knowledge comes in handy. Whether it's configuring shopping carts or using JavaScript libraries such as jQuery and Bootstrap, a little knowledge will make your life a whole lot easier. For just one example, Bootstrap makes use of JavaScript to easily resize and reposition text, images, and even video (among other things) depending on the size of the browser window—this is a very useful way of creating a responsive website.

Totem, well known for their beautiful innovative speakers, makes great use of minimalist design and responsive techniques with their new site.
Ref: http://www.totemacoustic.com

Besides the advantages in your everyday web design work, every time you learn something new, you elevate yourself. Learning basic programming will just make you a more valuable person to have around, which will be giving you more options in terms of the jobs you can take and the amount of money you can make—and there is nothing wrong with wanting to pay the bills!

What exactly is programming?

Let's start with the basics. Programming is basically talking to the computer in a language that it understands. And, just as humans have multiple spoken languages, so there are numerous programming languages that computers can speak. In a nutshell, programming languages allow you to give computers complex instructions. In the world of the Internet, the key language is arguably JavaScript.

But what exactly is a programming language? Well, like a spoken language, programming languages have rules—grammar, spelling, and so on—and meaning for certain special keywords.

In JavaScript, one such keyword is "function." This tells the computer that this is the start of programming code that does something, or in other words, takes an action. Here's a made-up example for JavaScript:

```
function: Pop up a box and say:
"What's up, Jimmy?"
```

This example (which is not real programming!) would be telling the computer to pop open a box and say: "What's up, Jimmy?"

Just for the curious, I will now show you the real way to do this with JavaScript:

```
function popupMessage()
{
alert("What's up, Jimmy?");
}
```

What's that supposed to mean? I know that for many of you this is already very confusing, but hold on, it's well worth it!

Programming languages have other words (besides "function") that have a special meaning that tells the computer what to do. So when you are programming, you are essentially just using keywords to tell the computer what to do.

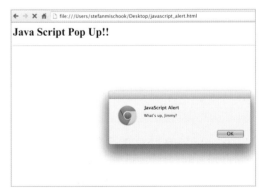

JavaScript "pop up" box in Chrome.

Programming languages allow you to write software (or in other words, build apps) and that software enables you to more easily control your computer.

The important thing to remember is that computers are really, really stupid. They are so stupid, in fact, that if you were talking to a computer directly, you would have to use a very simple language that is so slow to write that it would become very difficult to get anything done. This is because you would have to explain every single step to the computer.

How simple is the language needed? So simple that even something like displaying the letter "A" on screen could take you days because of all the code you would have to write!

The problem is, without the help of software or apps, computers can only understand "yes" and "no." If you go into a little more nerd detail, you will see that computers actually see "yes" and "no" as 1 and 0.

Because of how stupid computers really are, programmers have—over the years—written apps that make it much easier for us to "talk" to computers.

I hope that this basic explanation of programming clears things up a little— I've kept hitting the same basic points over and over again to be sure. That's still a lot of abstract information to take in, so let's take a look at something a little more concrete.

JavaScript, browsers, & programming

The JavaScript programming language is built into Firefox, Internet Explorer, Chrome, and all other web browsers. It allows us to really harness the power of web browsers in many ways that would not be possible otherwise. In fact, as we have said, JavaScript is an essential part of web design today.

Like many other programming languages, JavaScript is both a written language and an app that processes the code. So when I say "JavaScript is built into the web browsers," I simply mean the JavaScript app is part of the web browser.

Is HTML or CSS "programming?"

You know that HTML and CSS are used to give instructions to web browsers about what to display on a web page, and how to display it. To the uninitiated nerd, HTML and CSS may seem like programming languages, but they're not. So what is it that makes a "proper" programming language?

The fundamental difference between coding with HTML and CSS and programming is that in programming you can make decisions based on something happening.

As an example, you could write a little JavaScript that causes a small message box to appear if the user (the person looking at your page) does something. This could be clicking on a button or pressing a certain key on the keyboard, among other things. Of course, this is a simplified overview of the process, but it essentially covers it.

It can get confusing, though, because in the world of the Internet there can be "gray" areas where you can get the browser to do something on its own, without programming. An example of this is the "refresh" meta tag. This tag allows you to tell the web page to reload itself or to load an entirely new page after a specified number of seconds or minutes.

Here's what the "refresh" meta tag looks like:

```
<meta http-equiv='refresh'
content='3; URL=http://www.
studioweb.com'>
```

This tag tells the browser to load a page (in this instance "www.studioweb.com") after three seconds.

Meta tags are typically used to provide extra information about a web page that is not displayed in the page, such as the author of the page, a page description, or the last modified date. You place meta tags in the <head> section of a web page.

Now, you might think that because the meta tag code is telling the browser to do something, it is programming. Right? Wrong! The reason it is not programming is because there is no decision being made. No matter what else happens, the page will automatically load the website in the meta tag as long as the viewed stays on the initial web page for at least three seconds.

To make this example act as if it was truly programmed, you would have to add some sort of "decision" element to the process. An easy example would be to have a box on your web page where the user enters a number— depending on the number entered, the browser would load a particular page.

This simple example shows how programming allows you to make decisions based on as many possibilities you want.

One more example: you can, with JavaScript, check what time of the day it is. So with this information, you can send people to a particular website if it is, say, before 12 pm, or to send them to another web site if it is past 12 pm. Any combination is possible, thanks to programming!

Object-oriented programming

When learning something new, things may not be clear at first. However, push on, because sooner than you think, things will "snap" into place and soon you will be wondering why you thought all this programming stuff was so difficult!

One of the main reasons people find programming so challenging is that they do not get a good grasp of the basics. In my own process of learning to program (I have picked up nine languages so far) I have always found that every time I got confused it was because there was some basic concept I had not grasped fully. The solution is always to go back to the basics, because once you have them, everything else is easy!

Using the DOM

In advanced web design, your eventual goal is to use the DOM (the Document Object Model, talked about in the last chapter). This is the framework that allows you to have total control over your web pages using JavaScript.

What do I mean by "total control?" I am talking about being able to add, remove, and edit text, images, and tables—and any other element on the page—on the

fly; to easily build dynamic menus, change the font size of a paragraph on your page when someone clicks a link or image, and so on. I won't go on, but you can do all this (and much more) and it will work with all modern browsers, as the DOM is a standard that the browsers adhere to.

To be able to use the DOM effectively, you need to understand those pesky JavaScript basics I mentioned before. The good news is that the hard work of using the DOM has been made much easier thanks to the JavaScript libraries that are freely available. The most popular out there today is something called jQuery—I will be talking about jQuery in the second half of the book.

Nonetheless, you still need to know basic JavaScript programming concepts to use packages or libraries like jQuery, so let's look at the basics.

An example of a site using jQuery to stunning effect. Ref: http://ricardodelablanca.com

Object-oriented programming: the basics

Object-oriented programming (or OOP) is the "in" way to write software and is the foundation of many programming languages, including JavaScript. To understand how to use JavaScript, you must be familiar with some of the basic ideas of OOP.

I will only be teaching you what you need to know to be able to work with JavaScript, so don't worry about being overwhelmed! As an added bonus, what you learn about object-oriented programming here will apply to every object-oriented programming language out there—so you will be killing many birds with one stone.

OOP is the style of programming that is used in many of today's most prominent languages, including Java, PHP, C++, JavaScript, and several others. In a nutshell, OOP attempts to build programs by conceptually breaking them up into a series of individual objects (programmed objects) that work together to create a bigger program. In a sense, these objects are like mini apps inside one big app.

Another way you can think of it is as a business, where the business is the program and the objects are the people who work at the business: together, the people get the work done.

For example, let's say at a McDonalds we have Jamie (who works the cash), Stef (who makes the burgers), and Nick (who washes the floors). These three people are (in themselves) individual objects—this is a little insulting, I know, but this is just an example! Each of these guys (objects) has its own function (things that they do), but together they make the McDonalds work.

Of course, there are several other people working at McDonalds, but the point is that all these individuals work together to do the job of running the restaurant.

So, when you are object-oriented programming, you are creating a bunch of individual objects that work together to make the program as a whole. I will provide you with an example in just a minute, but before that, I have two questions that must be answered.

Firstly, what are the other ways of programming? The most prominent of the old styles of programming is procedural programming, where software was designed based on processes. OK, but what does that mean?

It means that the programmers who wrote the code for these apps structured the code in the order that they would do things—it was process driven. There's no need to go into greater detail because today you only need to learn OOP. The bottom line is that this old style of programming got messy really fast and resulted in buggy software that was (and still is) hard to maintain. OOP based software tries to solve this.

Secondly, why would you program the OOP way? You build software in the OOP style to save time and money: OOP-based software is easier to build and easier to maintain. Humans like to put things in boxes or categories to help organize them—OOP is essentially doing that.

Because JavaScript is built into every web browser (and is therefore essential in modern web design), we will delve deeper into programming concepts using JavaScript.

JavaScript objects

A web page contains many objects that you can manipulate with JavaScript. One of the base or foundation objects is the "window object." This object represents the browser window and provides many ways to affect changes to a browser's window using JavaScript.

Each object (inside the program) has things that it does. These "things" in programming-talk are called "functions." So, a function is essentially a thing that an object can do. Objects can potentially do many things, so you will often find objects with multiple functions.

OK, I don't want to confuse you, but I need to clarify something: functions can also be called "methods." Why do we call them functions or methods when they have the same meaning? The reason is simple: functions are different from methods! For our purposes, it is sufficient to say that when a function exists inside an object, it is called a "method."

I will not go beyond that explanation because to know the ultra-nerd details will have no impact on your ability to use JavaScript. The only reason I mention it is because when you start reading about JavaScript (and other OOP languages) you will see the word "method" used a lot.

The JavaScript alert function

One function (technically, a method) of the window object is "alert." Here is a simple example of how to actually use the alert function:

```
window.alert("This is an alert
box!");
```

This simple line has a lot of stuff going on. Once you understand what this line is actually doing, you will be well on your way to becoming a successful JavaScript programmer.

Keep in mind that since you are programming for use in a web browser, all of your programming code is being written to "talk" to the browser and tell it what to do.

In this example, the first line of code is telling the browser that you want to use the built-in "window" object—you do this by starting with the keyword "window."

Like most objects, the window object has built-in functions or methods. To tell the browser which method you want to use (inside the window object), you just name it. In this case, you want to use the "alert" method, so you type in a period after the keyword "window" and then the name of the method you want to use ("alert"):

```
window.alert
```

The period between the words "window" and "alert" acts like a pointer for the web browser, telling it that the second word ("alert") is a method inside the window object.

If you entered `window alert` without a period, the browser would have no idea what "alert" was about. In other words, the period between the words joins them together. This is called "dot notation" and is used a lot.

The next part of your line of code is much easier to understand:

```
("This is an alert box!");
```

All methods can be fed information that they can do something with—hold onto that thought. You feed the method this information by placing it inside the brackets ( ) that sit after the method name. In the above example we are feeding the alert method the text:

```
"This is an alert box!"
```

The browser knows it is text because "This is an alert box!" is sitting in between quotes (""). In programming, anything between quotes tells the computer that it is plain text.

When you feed a method or a function information in this way, it is called "passing arguments." In this example, the "argument" is the text, and you are "passing" it by placing it between brackets at the end of the method name:

```
window.alert("This is an alert
box!");
```

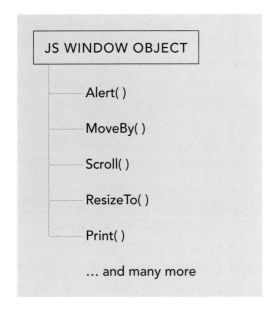

JS WINDOW OBJECT

- Alert( )
- MoveBy( )
- Scroll( )
- ResizeTo( )
- Print( )
- … and many more

More details about functions: the double brackets

At the end of every method or function in JavaScript you need to put two round brackets that face each other, so with the alert method you do this:

```
alert()
```

The two facing brackets at the end of a method or function, tell the browser that this is a method or function. It is also a good way for you to recognize functions when you see them—they always have a couple of brackets ( ) at the end. For example, the following are methods of the window object, or in other words, they are methods contained in the window object. Some programmers will say the same thing by saying: "alert ( ) belongs to the window object."

```
Open()
Close()
Focus()
```

There are several other methods that I have not listed—all you need to understand is that objects can have several built-in methods, and that methods are identified by placing a couple of round brackets after them.

You are now just about finished, except for one little thing. In JavaScript and several other languages, you need to tell the computer that it has reached the end of the line of programming code. To do this you use a semi-colon (;). In our example, this is the completed line:

```
window.alert("This is an alert box!");
```

Now, when the computer is reading this line it knows it is done when it finds the semi-colon.

OK, that's enough theory for now. Copy this code template into a blank HTML page (as before, you can download it from the book's website), and practice by changing the arguments passed to the alert method:

```html
<html>
<head>
<script language='javaScript'>
function callAlert() {
window.alert("This is an alert
box!");
}
</script>
</head>
<body>
<h3>Our first function</h3>
<a href='#' onClick='callAlert();
return false';>
Click here to call the function
</a>
</body>
</html>
```

Breaking down this code you will see that you created a function in the <head> of the page called "callAlert." This "calls" the built-in JavaScript alert function.

In the <body>, you have a hyperlink tag that uses the "onClick" attribute to activate/call the function "callAlert."

onClick is actually called an "event attribute," because it has to do with an event—in this case, clicking on the link. So, onClick can be read as: "on the click."

You will notice the text "return false:" on the link tag after the function call.

```html
<a href='#' onClick='callAlert();
return false';>
```

This tells the browser to stay on this page—it basically overrides the browser's default behavior.

The more you look at programming code—and the more you write it—the easier it becomes, so I would strongly suggest that you type it out by hand to get it to work, then change things and see how it breaks.

HTML event attributes

HTML is packed with event attributes that can all be accessed with JavaScript. For example: onclick, ondrag, onkeydown, and perhaps another 50 more. HTML event attributes are the key to turning websites into web apps.

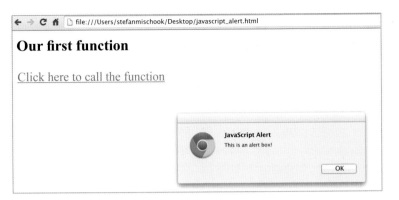

Using onClick to open a JavaScript alert box.

JavaScript frameworks

JavaScript has collections of JavaScript code organized into libraries, which are called "frameworks." There are several frameworks out there, but the most widely used is jQuery.

With HTML5 and CSS3, jQuery has replaced what people used to use Flash for. I am talking here about creating fancy layouts, special effects, embedding audio and video into web pages, and a whole lot more. Some of this will be covered in Part 2.

Why did we look at JavaScript?

You've reached the end of your study of programming (that wasn't so hard!) and although you can hardly call yourself a programmer, you should now have an understanding of some of the key programming concepts. Now, when someone talks about "objects" or "functions" you will hopefully know what's going on, and when you start to use some of the popular JavaScript libraries, such as jQuery, you will have a much easier time with it. Finally, if you decide to take the plunge and get into serious JavaScript (or maybe some PHP), you will have a foundation to build on.

CHAPTER 7

Essential Background Knowledge

Learning web design is like painting walls—it is best done in layers. Anyone who has painted walls before knows that you need more than one layer of paint to get a good finish, and the same applies to learning web design.

This chapter will revisit some of the subjects we covered earlier, but I will now fill in some of the gaps so you have a deeper, more complete understanding of what is going on.

Some of you might be asking, "Why didn't you cover it to start with?" but I've found that if you throw too much at someone at the same time, it just gets too confusing—small bytes! Yes, I misspelled bites on-purpose.

As I've mentioned, the better you understand the basics, the easier the more advanced topics will be. By the end of this chapter you will be more than ready to tackle Part 2 of this book, where we get into fancier, more advanced web design.

Understanding how web browsers process HTML, CSS, and JavaScript will not only help you as you learn, but also help you in your future work. Many bugs and glitches can be solved with a deeper knowledge of the inner workings of browsers.

Browser rendering engines

Web browsers are equipped with mini programs called "rendering engines," which read and execute whatever it is that the HTML, CSS, and JavaScript code is telling them to do.

- Apple's Safari uses the WebKit engine.

- Google's Chrome used to use WebKit, but now uses another version of WebKit called WebCore.

- Firefox uses the Gecko engine.

There are more rendering engines and browsers (Internet Explorer and Opera, for example), some of which share the same engines, while others use their own. But why should you care?

The existence of multiple rendering engines explains why your code might work in one web browser, but not in another. This still happens, even though the specification for how the code should be processed is set by the W3C.

What is the W3C?

The W3C is basically the group of companies and individuals who come up with the specifications for the web. They set how HTML, CSS, and JavaScript should work, and how web browsers should render the code. Yet while they set the rules, not everyone plays by them, which has caused web designers heartache over the years, and me to lose 20% of my hair!

Browser top-down processing

Before you yawn and fall asleep, the next few paragraphs are super important—it's just a page, so pay attention!

When a web browser loads a page, it starts to read it from the top of the page of code and works its way down. This may not seem like an important thing now, but this top-down method of processing web pages plays a major role in day-to-day web design work.

For example, let's say you were using a big JavaScript library to help create some nifty animations on your page. Because the JavaScript library can take a little more time to load, it makes sense to put it at the bottom of your page, so the rest of the page loads first, giving the user something to see while the library loads in the background.

This is just a simple example, but what you need to take away is that browsers start reading the code for a web page from the top and work their way down the code to the bottom.

As the browser reads the page, it loads the information into its own memory. Any special effects that happen after the page loads (like clicking on a dynamic menu,

for example), come from the browser working with the code stored in its memory—the original page it read is not changed at all.

Therefore, the HTML, CSS, and JavaScript code you wrote serves only as a template of sorts for the browser to use.

That might not make sense right now, but in time it will sink in, and it will help you solve bugs down the road. A lot of active web designers don't understand this at all!

```
1  <!DOCTYPE html>
2  <html>
3  <head>
4  <title>Chapter 8 CSS Tutorial - Liquid Layout</title>
5  <meta charset="UTF-8">
6  <link href="chapter-8-liquid.css" rel="stylesheet"
7  </head>
8
9  <body>
10
11 <div id="container">
12
13 <div id="header">
14
15 <h1>The Page Header</h1>
16
17 </div>
18
19 <div id="navigation">
20      <!--<h2>The Main Navigation</h2>
21      <ul>
22          <li><a href=#>Home</a></li>
23          <li><a href=#>Store</a></li>
24          <li><a href=#>Blog</a></li>
25          <li><a href=#>Contact Us</a></li>
26      </ul>
27 </div>
28
29 <div id="centreDoc">
30      <img id="miamiBuilding" src="miami.png"
    height="350" width="193">
```

Browsers read the code on a web page from the top downward.

Web frameworks

What are web frameworks, and why should you care? In a nutshell, a web framework is a library of code that you can simply insert into your own web pages. The goal of these frameworks is to speed up the web design process and reduce the amount of bugs and errors in your pages.

In modern web design, there are many frameworks to choose from, including:

• Twitter Bootstrap
• jQuery
• Foundation Framework
• Sass
• Compass

There are many, many more, but only a couple (in my opinion) are essential today: Twitter Bootstrap and jQuery. In Part 2 we will take a closer look at this dynamic duo.

Frameworks speed up the web design process because the code is already written and the bugs smashed. For example, you could spend hours tweaking the code for a drop-down menu to ensure that it works in all standard browsers and on iPhones, iPads, and Android devices.

Or you could simply drop in a Bootstrap menu and be done in minutes—the choice is simple!

Frameworks also reduce the amount of bugs, as the code is typically very refined—frameworks have been tested, retested, and worked on by probably thousands of web designers and programmers. If a framework has, say, 20,000 coding hours of work put into it, it will almost always be better than anything you could produce on your own!

Now for my (perhaps) controversial position when it comes to web frameworks:

I've always been a big advocate of taking advantage of frameworks, although there will always be a class of web developers and designers who hate leaving the old-school ways of doing things behind. For example, when the Java programming language come out in the 1990s, it was much maligned by the C programming guys, because it was too high level for their taste. Yet today, Java is one of the most used programming languages out there.

Apple made a similar move with the iPhone, when it said no more hard keyboards, and also with the MacBook Air where it said no more optical drives. Some people howled in protest, but we know what happened there!

So, I am sure there will be some nerds out there who will be annoyed that I am advocating that you should almost always use frameworks. Yes, you still need to understand the basic mechanics of HTML, CSS, and JavaScript, but there's no point wasting your time when there are all these great tools out there. In web design, tools = web frameworks, and web frameworks are power tools!

Be ready to change!

As this suggests, you should be ready and willing to use new web design tools and technologies. That doesn't mean you should jump on every new thing that comes out (you will not have the time!) but you should keep an open mind and be ready to casually explore them and use them *when it makes sense*. Every once in a while, something like Bootstrap or jQuery comes along!

One of many sites that takes advantage of web frameworks to create a modern responsive website.
Ref: http://www.verenamichelitsch.com

Designing websites for tablets & smartphones

Recent studies show that 30% of the web's traffic is on mobile devices. Needless to say, this means you need to build websites that work well on smartphones and tablets. There are a few ways to handle this, but it essentially comes down to two things:

1. Build your websites so that they change or respond to the device that is visiting it—this is called "responsive" web design. You can do this with JavaScript and CSS, or build your websites using Bootstrap, which will take care of it for you.

2. Have a programmer build a native, dedicated app for mobile devices ("native" means in the native language of the mobile device). This means you would have to build one for iOS (iPhones and iPads), one for Android devices, one for Windows phones, and one for the 12 people who use a Blackberry!

This, of course, goes beyond the scope of a web design book, but I can offer some practical advice: for most websites, you don't need to build a native dedicated app—a responsive website works great most of time.

Vogue uses Bootstrap with its visually stunning site. Ref: http://www.vogue.fr

The client-server model

You may have heard the term "client-server" before—the term is out there and it's pretty popular among the nerds. But why?

First of all, client-server refers to client and server computers—something we talked about in Chapter 1.

Websites and web apps are all about the client-server model or style of distributed computing. Distributed? This means you have two or more computers involved in doing some job or calculation.

For example, think about a simple shopping cart. In this scenario you have the client computer picking items in the store and you have the server computer tracking all the items that are placed in the shopping cart. This means you have two computers distributing the work between themselves.

When your websites start doing things—such as taking orders via a shopping cart, for example, or allowing users to subscribe to a newsletter or to a blog—your site has graduated from a basic website to a web app. These days, the line between websites and web apps is fading quickly, as most websites need

some sort of functionality. "Brochure" websites that are just a bunch of pages with text and images are far less common.

Now consider this: of the top one million websites, roughly 80% use the server-side programming language PHP. However, there are a lot of other competing languages to PHP, including Ruby, Java, Python, C#, and more.

The point is, as a web designer you will likely run into web app related work where you will have to work with web programmers (sometimes called "web developers"), so it is good to know the basic lay of the land, if you will. And now you do!

Client vs. server

Client computers are so named because they are on the receiving end of an information transaction between two computers. The computer that gets the information is the client, and the computer that is sending it out is the server.

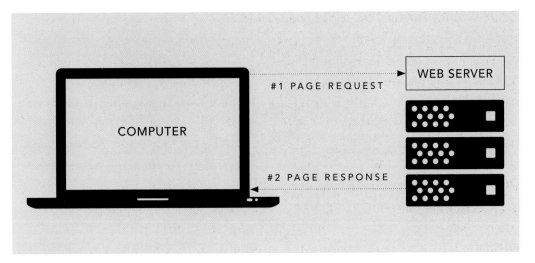

COMPUTER

#1 PAGE REQUEST

WEB SERVER

#2 PAGE RESPONSE

A computer sends a "client request"
and the server responds.

The request-response cycle

When you go to a website, your computer (in the background, through the web browser) is sending a message to the server that is hosting the web site. That message is called a "client request," because your computer is considered the "client" computer and is literally requesting to see the server's files (in this case, web page files).

The request-response cycle is basically a process of communication between a client computer and a server computer (as shown in the diagram above). It's like a client at a restaurant requesting to see the menu. In our restaurant analogy, the waiter is the server, bringing the menu to the client.

How is this important to new web designers? Because understanding the underlying structure of the web (including the request-response cycle) will help you as a web designer. Over the years, I've experienced the benefits of this seemingly obscure bit of knowledge, and I know you will as well. Just keep it in mind and one day something will pop up that will make you glad you understand this.

Client-side vs. server-side languages

Now that you know the difference between a client computer and a server computer, I imagine you can guess the differences between client-side languages and server-side languages (hint: the latter runs on the server).

I've mentioned a few popular server-side languages: PHP, Ruby, Java, Python, and C#. There are more, but these are the most popular.

Server-side languages are basically the engine of all web apps: Facebook, Twitter, and Amazon all rely heavily on server-side programming, for example. You use the server-side language to capture user information (typically via web forms), store various information in databases, and do all kinds of manipulation of this information (and much more).

I mention these languages because there is a very good chance that as a web designer you will at some point have to work with web apps.

Web designers who work on web apps don't necessarily need to know server-side programming, but they do need to understand the basics of how it works and should be able to provide pages that are well structured and properly coded. You are learning the basics of this here.

The good news is that the only client-side language you need to be concerned about is JavaScript. This is a client-side language because the JavaScript code is processed by the web browser.

Front end and back end

These are terms that you will hear regularly in the web design and development world.

"Front end" is referencing client-side web development and design, while "back end" is talking about server-side programming. So if a web developer said "We are still working on the front end this week," that would mean the work's being done on the client-side.

The blurring roles of web designers and programmers

The separation between web designers and web programmers is blurring. These days, the web designer who can only design is going the way of the dodo bird—they are disappearing. Check out the evolution of the web designer:

1994

If a web designer knew basic HTML and could upload a nice photograph they were considered a guru!

1997

Web designers made heavy use of programs like Photoshop to design websites and then exported them to WYSIWYG web design software like Dreamweaver or Frontpage. Having good knowledge of code was secondary, so web designers and programmers had very different roles.

2003

Web designers now had to have a good knowledge of HTML (XHTML) and CSS code. More importantly, they had to understand the details about coding, proper page structure, and so on.

Today

Web designers not only have to know HTML and CSS, but also need at least a basic understanding of JavaScript. Modern web designers are increasingly evolving into web developers who concentrate on the client—in other words: client-side web developers.

Why so many server-side programming languages?

Mostly because of competition, but also sometimes because someone somewhere figures there is a better way of doing things.

So which is the best server-side programming language? In my experience, I find all the major languages are neck and neck in terms of capabilities—everything has its good and bad. So which is best comes down to a matter of taste. That said, around 80% of websites run PHP, so there is plenty more work around for competent PHP coders!

What is web usability?

Basically, usability is both a process and a measure of the ease of use of a website. In other words, web usability is:

1. A set of rules and principles you can apply to make web sites easier to use.

2. A measure of how easy a site is to use.

We've all visited websites where we're not sure which images are buttons; have no idea where to search for something; or find the menus are confusing and don't take us where we expect to go. These are all examples of bad web usability. Web usability is something all web designers should have a basic knowledge of.

Making a website more usable

The process of making a website more user-friendly forces you to look at:

• Colors used in the website. Dark colors, for example, are not good for sales!

• The fonts used.

• The placement of buttons and menus.

• The words you use.

• The choice of images used.

If you haven't guessed it already, web usability has a lot to do with basic human psychology and how our brains work. Web usability is a whole field unto itself and there are specialized web designers who are "usability experts" They command a high price!

My top web usability rules

Entire books have been written on usability, but if you follow these simple rules you will have gone a long way toward making a site user-friendly:

• Keep your layouts consistent across pages. The website's navigation bars should be the same (in terms of the menu items) and should fall in the same place on the pages in your website. If you have a navigation bar at the top of the homepage, for example, be sure to have navigation at the top of all your other pages as well.

• The homepage should make it clear what the site is about.

• Don't cram your pages up. Leave space so that pages are easy to read. When you first come to a website, it should feel relaxing, not confusing or frustrating.

- Typically, links should look the same across all pages. Don't have green underlined links on one page and then bold blue text (with no underlines) for your links on another. If your links don't look the same, people will miss them.

- Scrolling is OK (although it is not ideal on some sites), but sideways scrolling is usually best avoided! Scrolling should be limited to the vertical axis (up and down).

- The website's logo should always be a link to the homepage. This is one of the oldest rules in the web design book—it is now almost instinctive for people to click on a logo to go to the homepage

- Use terms that are common and make sense. For example, the "Contact us" page should be called exactly that, rather than "Correspondence."

- Keep paragraphs short and make liberal use of sub headings to break up the content. People scan web pages.

- Become aware of web conventions. For example, menus are at the top of pages and the sides; content runs in the middle of the page; and the footer contains links to key pages such as "About" and "Contact us."

Sony makes excellent use of a technique called parallax scrolling, where the background moves at a slower rate than the foreground, creating a slick 3D effect as you scroll down the page. Ref: http://www.sony.com/be-moved

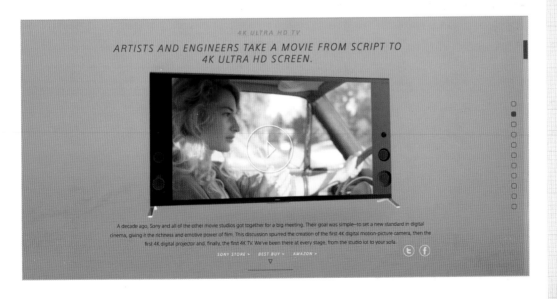

• Use lists when you have more than three items. So, rather than:

My favorite foods: cake, cheese, bacon, raisins, beer, tacos, fries, and salmon cakes.

... Go with:

My Favorite Foods:

cake

cheese

bacon

raisins

beer

tacos

fries

salmon cakes

Plenty of white space, a logo linked to the homepage, and a consistent menu are cardinal rules of good usability. Ref: https://www.interactivered.com

Where to learn more

The king of usability is Jakob Nielsen, who runs the Nielsen Norman Group. They study usability and provide great articles and research data. Check it out at:

http://www.nngroup.com/articles

WordPress, Drupal, & Joomla—how they fit into modern web design

WordPress, Drupal, and Joomla are free (and competing) content management systems, which are very popular these days. Most of the time people just call them a CMS (Content Management System). This is a piece of software that you install on a server, which then allows the creation, publishing, and editing of content (text, images, and video) that is delivered as a website. You can think of them as "super blogs."

One of my tutorial sites—csstutorial.net—is an example of an entire website created in WordPress. However, there is nothing that tells you WordPress is operating behind the scenes—as far as anyone is concerned, this is just a "normal" website.

However, the minute I log in as an administrator, WordPress automatically gives me a nifty editor bar at the top of all the pages. This lets me navigate around the site and if I want to make changes to any pages, I just have to click on the top "Edit Page" link and that takes me to a pretty good text editor—as shown on the screenshot over the page.

WordPress websites come in every shape and size, and can be nearly impossible to spot. Ref: http://www.kylie.com

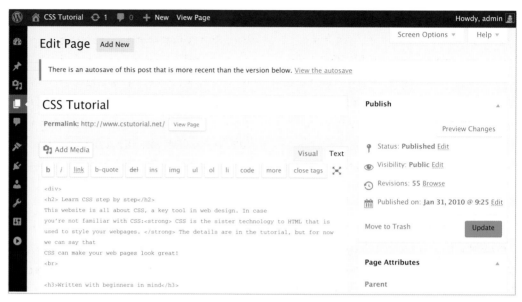

WordPress comes with a built-in text editor that is very easy to use.

Using a CMS to create a website is very popular these days because when you use a CMS you get all kinds of extra functionality for free. A CMS makes creating and editing web pages almost like using a word processor—no coding skills are required and no FTP is required to upload images and new files. Instead, it is all handled by the CMS software, which stores all the information that is displayed on the website.

WordPress, the most popular of the three, runs about 18% of websites! As a web designer, you might be called on to work with one of these products—in fact, there are very successful web designers out there who work almost exclusively with

The major CMS options

The three major CMS options are:
WordPress: http://WordPress.org
Joomla: http://www.joomla.org
Drupal: http://www.drupal.org

any one of these three CMS options, as they are that popular.

Web designers hired to work on a CMS-based site will typically be faced with two major tasks:

1. Installing and configure the CMS.
2. Creating the visual templates.

When you are creating a CMS template, you are basically designing the front end which is built with HTML, CSS, and JavaScript. The difference between the coding done on a normal website versus a CMS-based site is that you have to structure your code (HTML, CSS, and possibly JavaScript) around the server-side code used in the CMS.

This is yet another example of how important it is to know a little bit about programming; if you don't understand basic programming, then working with a CMS to create templates can be a pain.

Summary of the differences between the CMS options

Each of these apps is very complex and you will get nerd-battles over which is best. I've worked with WordPress for years and have installed and configured Drupal a few times in the past.

WordPress

WordPress started out as a simple blog engine and over the years it has had more and more features added to it. It has now become a much more powerful system and has graduated from blog to full-blown CMS. It's still not nearly as powerful as Drupal or Joomla, but it is a lot easier to learn!

WordPress has the advantage of being easy to install and there is a huge number of ready-made templates that you can get either for free, as well as commercial templates at a reasonable price—many are under $50 USD. You can also find WordPress templates that offer much more than the visual component— some offer extra functionality as well.

WordPress also has plugin capabilities, so programmers can extend its basic features. There is now a huge collection

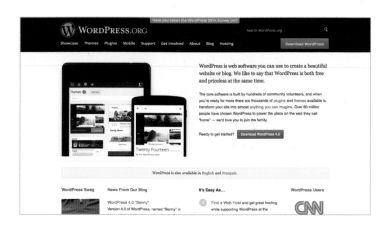

https://wordpress.org is the place to go to download WordPress.

of plugins to choose from, including shopping carts, forums, chat systems, polling systems, and more.

The downside to using WordPress is that it is open to attack. It is notoriously "hackable" and many WordPress sites have been infiltrated—my own included! However, WordPress has recently included an auto-update feature, which should quickly close any security holes that people discover—the biggest problem at the moment is people not keeping WordPress up to date.

Drupal & Joomla
Both Drupal and Joomla started life as a CMS, and it shows. They are far more powerful than WordPress and can do a lot more. However, the cost of this power is complexity. Both offer the same sort of "ecosystem" as WordPress, but they are not nearly as popular. While Drupal and Joomla have large communities supplying templates, plugins, and support, they still pale in size relative to WordPress.

Installing a CMS
WordPress, Drupal, and Joomla are created in PHP, and so to be able to install them you need a PHP-enabled server. Thankfully, just about every hosting company has PHP servers, and there is no extra cost for it. Besides PHP, you also need a MySQL database which the CMS will use to store all its information. Again,

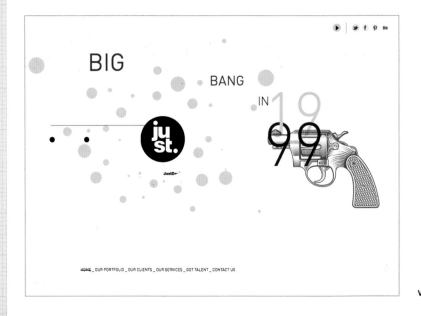

This South African branding agency website uses Drupal (as well as a whole lot of cool effects). Ref: http://www.justdesign.co.za

there are no worries on that front, either—if a hosting company supports PHP, you will get MySQL as well.

Entire books have been written on each of these CMS options, so there isn't space to go over everything here. What I will do, though, is provide a quick run through of the basic process of installing WordPress, so you have an idea of how it works.

A quicker install

Your hosting company may already have a one-click install of WordPress, in which case you don't need to do anything except click the button to install it inside your hosting account's control panel. Ask your host if they have this.

Installing WordPress

1. Go to WordPress.org and download the install files (1). You will have the option to download either a .zip version or a .tar.gz version. The simple solution—whether you're using Windows or Mac—is to download the .zip version.

2. The downloader will drop a folder called "WordPress" wherever you told it to put the download. (I always put things on my desktop so they are easy to find.) If you open that folder you will

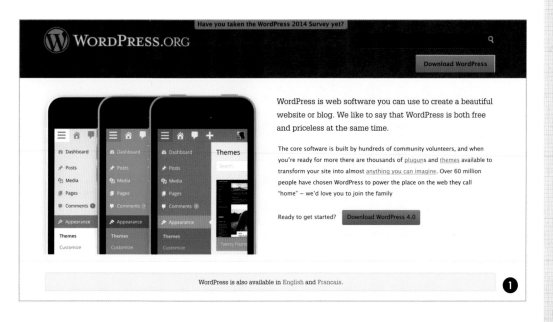

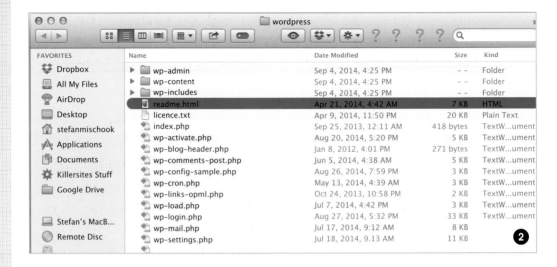

find a bunch of PHP pages and some more subdirectories—as you can see in the screenshot (2). Open the file called "readme.html" to see instructions on how to set it all up.

3. Next, you will need to set up your MySQL database on your server. In cPanel (a very popular control panel used by hosting companies) you simply go to the "MySQL Databases" configuration page and create a new database (3). Once this has been created, copy the database connection details. You will need:

- database name
- user name
- password

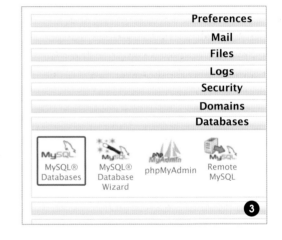

4. Once you have your database connection details, return to the WordPress folder and open the file called "wp-config-sample.php" using a code editor. Toward the top of the page you will need to enter in the database connection details:

```
/** The name of the database
for WordPress */
define('DB_NAME', 'database_name_
here');
/** MySQL database username */
define('DB_USER', 'username_here');
/** MySQL database password */
define('DB_PASSWORD', 'password_
here');
/** MySQL hostname */
define('DB_HOST', 'localhost');
```

For example, in the first line you see the text "database_name_here"—just replace that text with the database name. For example, if your database had the name "my_wordpress_database," you would change the code to:

```
define('DB_NAME', 'my_wordpress_
database');
```

The rest of the configuration settings are completed in the same way. Once this is done, upload all the WordPress files to your hosting account where you complete the installation. The readme document will guide you through the process.

The WordPress nerds like to call the installation process the "famous five-minute install," but in my experience it will probably take you around 20 minutes (unless you are an uber-nerd already), as have to set up your MySQL database on the server as well.

Which CMS should you choose and do you need to learn one at all?

Do you have to learn any of these CMS options to become a web designer? Not at all! But you should be aware that they are out there and are a fact of life in modern web design.

If you are interested in learning one, then I would suggest WordPress, as it is the most popular. I am not saying WordPress is the best (each has its pros and cons), but it is far more likely you will end up working with WordPress than you will any of the other two (or any of the many other CMS options that are out there).

Having said that, Drupal and Joomla are better suited for big sites, so go with one of these if you imagine you will have a huge site with many administrators and subsections that will have to look and respond differently.

CHAPTER 8

CSS Layouts

In Chapter 4, I used a simple layout as a way to introduce CSS to you in a practical way. However, that barely scratched the surface, so in this chapter—with your growing skills—you are going to dive deep into creating layouts in CSS.

Page layout with CSS is probably the trickiest part of web design. Fortunately, if you follow a few simple rules you can avoid all the major headaches.

There are four basic CSS layout styles that we will briefly look at. You will then see how you can apply two of them to the basic page you built in Chapter 4, when you were still a web design novice.

The Chapter 4 web page had a very straightforward layout, as its purpose was to demonstrate basic CSS concepts and techniques. Now that you are getting pretty good at this web design stuff, you are going to put together a production-quality web layout structure.

First, let's quickly cover the four basic CSS layout styles, which are:

1. Static design
2. Liquid design
3. Adaptive design
4. Responsive design

1. Static design

The web site layout you constructed in Chapter 4 was a primitive example of a static design. It's called a static design because you used pixels to set the size of the page and the navigation and center document sections.

Whenever you use pixels, you are basically setting the size in stone. If the user resizes the window to make it smaller, the page will not shrink—it will simply get cut off. Conversely, if they have a large, high-resolution monitor, the web page will not expand. There is a good side to this and a bad side. The advantage of a static design is that you have maximum control over how the page appears; the disadvantage is that the page won't fit perfectly for a lot of visitors.

2. Liquid design

As the name suggests, liquid layouts flow with the size of the visitor's browser window. So, if someone has a very high resolution monitor and stretches their browser window wide, a liquid layout will stretch out to fill that. The opposite is also true—as the browser window is shrunk, a liquid layout will shrink as well. There are two things I should mention here: first, you do have control over how much it expands or contracts, but secondly, it isn't perfect—sometimes there is too much shrinkage, and it's not possible to compensate with a liquid design alone.

3. Adaptive design

This is a type of pixel-based layout that also uses a new capability found in CSS3: media queries. CSS3 media queries allow you to detect how big the web browser window is, and adjust these dimensions on the fly. You will learn more about this in Chapter 11.

4. Responsive design

This is the most advanced and flexible layout style. It combines both liquid layouts and CSS3 media queries. Today, this is the style many web designers are leaning toward because it provides the best of both worlds.

In this chapter you are going to take your page from Chapter 4 and transform it first into a proper static design, and then into a liquid design. In doing this you will learn some nuanced aspects of CSS layout, as well as some new general CSS skills.

A quick comment about Bootstrap: Bootstrap makes laying out the best possible pages a dream, and I suspect that worrying about raw CSS techniques for page layout will eventually be a thing of the past. That said, it's still a good idea to learn the basic techniques, as most websites continue to use them. Besides, Bootstrap is just doing this behind the scenes, and it is always good to know how things work under the hood.

Building a static CSS layout

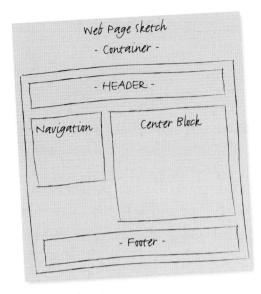

A sketch of the page you are looking to build.

The best place to start is to look at your bare-bones HTML code. I am going to strip out the extra text (with the exception of a few <p> tags) and just leave the HTML structural <div> tags in place:

```
<!DOCTYPE html>
<html>
<head>
<title>Ch8 CSS Tutorial - Fixed
Pixel Layout</title>
<meta charset="UTF-8">
<link href="chapter-8-static.css"
rel="stylesheet">
</head>
<body>
<div id=»container»>
<div id="header">
<p>header</p>
</div>
<div id="navigation">
<p>navigation</p>
</div>
<div id="centerDoc">
<p>center document</p>
</div> <!-- ends centerDoc-->
<div id="footer">
<p>footer</p>
</div>
</div> <!-- ends container-->
</body>
</html>
```

When you look at the page as it currently stands (1), you can see it looks very plain. This is because you have yet to write the

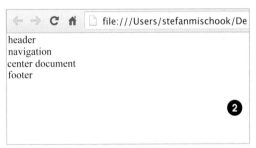

The page as rendered by the browser at this stage.

CSS code in your attached external style sheet—chapter-8-static.css (this can be downloaded from the book's website).

The star selector (*)

Let's start at the top of your CSS page, where you will add a CSS selector you have not seen before:

```
*  {
margin: 0;
padding: 0;
}
```

This star selector (*) is actually called the "universal selector," because it selects everything on your pages. Here this selector is setting the padding and margins of everything on the page to 0.

Why are you doing this? Because some web browsers have different default settings for the padding and margins.

This inconsistency between browsers has been a source of frustration for many web designers—your author included!

If you think about it, you want to be pixel perfect when laying out your pages. If you are off by just one pixel, everything can shift and your whole layout can get screwed up.

So, if one web browser decides that the <body> should have an invisible 1 pixel border around it, but another sets it to 2 pixels, your layouts are burnt toast. By using the universal star selector, you even the playing field, avoiding this hassle. Check out what happens to your page once this bit of CSS code is applied (2).

Notice how the text no longer has any margins and is pressed right up to touch the browser window.

The #container <div>

One of the things that is different about this page's code, compared to the page in Chapter 4, is the use of a <div> that wraps around all the other tags in the <body> of the page.

This <div> has an ID of "container" and this container <div> will contain all of the layout code. Having a container <div> will allow you to set a page width (in pixels) and it will also enable you to easily center your page. This is the CSS code for the container <div>:

```
#container {
width:960px;
margin-top:10px;
margin-right:auto;
margin-left:auto;
margin-bottom:10px;
position:relative;
background-color:#FFF;
}
```

Note that the width in the #container CSS is set to 960px. This is because—at the time of writing—960 pixels is a pretty good width that the vast majority of people's computer screens can handle. Most of the rest of the CSS code in this #container ID is stuff you've seen before, so let's concentrate on new CSS.

Browser stats

It's always a good idea to know the trends regarding web surfer statistics, such as the browsers being used, operating systems, and screen resolutions. There are many places to go to get this data, but a good site is the W3C: http://www.w3schools.com/browsers/browsers_display.asp

First there is this:

```
margin-right:auto;
margin-left:auto;
```

This code centers the container <div> horizontally, with the value "auto" telling the web browser to automatically calculate the space that is left over at the left and the right of the #container <div>.

The #container <div> is also set to "position: relative," as you are using things called "floats" in your CSS. With "position," you have two options—"relative" and "absolute"—but if you use floats in your layouts, you have to use "position:relative." (Don't worry, I'll explain floats in just a moment.)

The #header div

Now let's add the #header CSS code:

```
#header {
background-color: #FAF0E6;
margin-bottom: 20px;
border-style: solid;
border-width: 1px;
border-color: red;
}
```

This is pretty standard stuff, so let's move on quickly.

The #navigation, #centerDoc, and #footer divs

With all three of these <div>s, some new CSS is being used—the "float" property. So what does "float" do? Well, it floats a tag left or right. In this example, you want the navigation at the left side of the page (see the page sketch on page 140), so the navigation <div> is set to float left:

```
#navigation {
float: left;
width: 198px;
background-color:#FAF0E6;
border-style: solid;
border-width: 1px;
border-color: red;
}
```

As the #container <div> has a width of 960px, you need to fit your #navigation and #centerDoc within that, otherwise things will shift.

I figured the #navigation <div> should have 200px and the #centerDoc <div>, 760px/ However, you will notice in the code that the #navigation <div> has a width of 198px, which is two pixels less than the 200px planned. Why is this? Because #navigation also has a 1px border width. As there is a left and a right side, this adds two pixels to the width of your #navigation <div> (198 + 2 = 200).

Important CSS layout tip!

With web page layouts you have to be pixel perfect when it comes to the horizontal axis—the left and right sides. Never change the padding, borders, or margins to the left or right of structural divs to tweak the positioning of things, as this can throw your whole page layout off. Instead, apply padding or margins to elements (tags) inside the containers.

With regard to the width and borders of #centerDoc, the exact same considerations apply. Here is the #centerDoc <div> code:

```
#centerDoc {
float: right;
width: 738px;
background-color:#FAF0E6;
margin-left: 20px;
border-style: solid;
border-width: 1px;
border-color: red;
}
```

With #centerDoc, the float is to the right and it's got margin-left set at 20px. This means you have to add that 20 pixel margin when you are doing the math to be sure everything fits in your #container <div>.

Finally, #footer is also floated to the right, but you do something new to push it underneath all the other divs in the page: you use a CSS property called "clear."

This code—clear: both;—basically tells the browser to push this <div> clear past any other <div>s in the page.

This results in it being pushed to the footer of the page, which is where you want it to be:

```
#footer {
float: right;
width: 738px;
clear: both;
background-color: #FAF0E6;
margin-top: 20px;
margin-left: 20px;
border-style: solid;
border-width: 1px;
border-color: red;
}
```

I set the width of the #footer to 738px because I didn't want it to extend under the navigation. That was just a design decision on my part—you could just as easily set it to 958px.

You may have noticed that with the #header <div>, you did not have to set a width. This is because <div>s are block elements, so they naturally extend across the total width of the available space. However, in this case the #footer is floated, so you have to specify a width. If not, it will act like an inline tag and won't extend the width of the page.

Wow, the page structure is done! If you look at the page now (3), you will see how the <div>s are nicely positioned.

It still doesn't look like much, but it will very soon—the hard part is done!

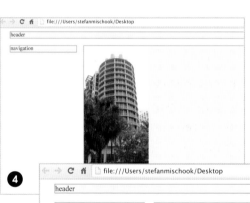

Positioning an image

OK, let's stick an image into your HTML page, inside the #centerDoc:

```
<div id="centerDoc">
<img id="miamiBuilding" src="miami.
png" height="350" width="193">
</div> <!-- ends centerDoc-->
```

The Miami building photo is not in the best spot (4), so let's add this CSS code:

```
#miamiBuilding {
float: right;
margin: 20px;
}
```

That's better (5)!

More about floats

When you apply a "float" to a tag, you basically take that tag out of the natural page-flow—it floats up above the page. It helps to think of it as a balloon floating above a room.

Special thanks to KillerSites Andrea for that analogy.

Much of the rest of the code is CSS and HTML that you've seen before. If you haven't already, you can download the full code from the book's website. Then, with the text put in place, your humble HTML page will look like a proper web page!

Positioning text

As you can see in the screenshot below (6), the text is all squished up at the moment and the list has the numbers hanging out over the edge of the #centerDoc <div>, which is not ideal.

You could add some padding or margins to the #centerDoc <div>, but look what happens if you add 20px of padding to the #centerDoc <div>—the whole div shifts (7)!

As noted previously, you should never touch the padding, margins, or borders of your structural <div> tags to adjust the position of elements inside them. Instead, the solution is to add padding to the tags *inside* the container <div>s.

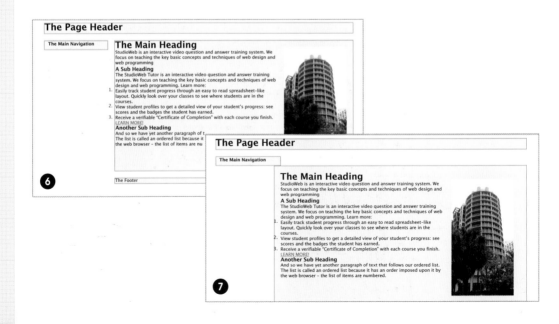

This is the CSS that solves the problem (8):

```
#header h1 {
padding: 10px;
}
#centerDoc p, h3, h1{
padding-left: 10px;
padding-right: 10px;
}
#centerDoc p {
margin-bottom: 10px;
}
#centerDoc h1, h3 {
margin-bottom: 10px;
}
#centerDoc li {
list-style: none;
padding-left: 10px;
```

```
line-height: 1.5em;
}
#centerDoc ol{
margin-bottom: 10px;
}
#footer p {
padding: 10px;
}
```

OK, the page you've created isn't the most beautiful in the world, but the goal here is that you understand how to build solid, well-coded pages.

Using the CSS code list-style: none (we removed the numbered bullets in the #centerDoc <div>).

The Page Header

The Main Navigation

The Main Heading

StudioWeb is an interactive video question and answer training system. We focus on teaching the key basic concepts and techniques of web design and web programming

A Sub Heading

The StudioWeb Tutor is an interactive video question and answer training system. We focus on teaching the key basic concepts and techniques of web design and web programming. Learn more:

Easily track student progress through an easy to read spreadsheet-like layout. Quickly look over your classes to see where students are in the courses.

View student profiles to get a detailed view of your student's progress: see scores and the badges the student has earned.
Receive a verifiable "Certificate of Completion" with each course you finish.
LEARN MORE!

Another Sub Heading

And so we have yet another paragraph of text that follows our ordered list. The list is called an ordered list because it has an order imposed upon it by the web browser - the list of items are numbered.

The Footer

8

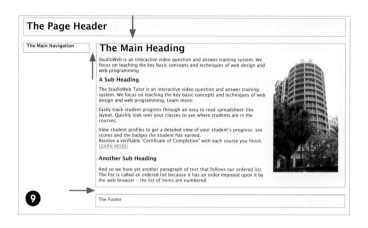

The Page Header

The Main Navigation

The Main Heading

StudioWeb is an interactive video question and answer training system. We focus on teaching the key basic concepts and techniques of web design and web programming

A Sub Heading

The StudioWeb Tutor is an interactive video question and answer training system. We focus on teaching the key basic concepts and techniques of web design and web programming. Learn more:

Easily track student progress through an easy to read spreadsheet-like layout. Quickly look over your classes to see where students are in the courses.

View student profiles to get a detailed view of your student's progress: see scores and the badges the student has earned.
Receive a verifiable "Certificate of Completion" with each course you finish.
LEARN MORE!

Another Sub Heading

And so we have yet another paragraph of text that follows our ordered list. The list is called an ordered list because it has an order imposed upon it by the web browser – the list of items are numbered.

The Footer

Space between the page sections

You may have noticed that your layout has a 20px space between the major sections of the page (9). So, between #navigation <div> and #centerDoc <div> there is a 20px space, and there's a 20px space between #centerDoc <div> and #footer <div>. I put in these spaces so you could clearly see the <div>s on the page—hopefully it will help you to understand what you are doing.

These spaces were inserted using CSS margins. For example, inside the #centerDoc CSS you will find:

```
margin-left: 20px;
```

That is the code that created the space between the main navigation menu and #centerDoc. Of course, any extra space needs to be factored into your page calculations when you first put together the structure for the page.

If you recall, 960px was the width of the #container <div>, so for this layout the math was:

(#centerDoc width: 738px) + (20px left margin) + (2px #centerDoc borders) + (198px #navigation) + (2px #navigation borders) = 960px

Creating a navigation menu

The only thing that's left is to build a navigation menu, which can be done with HTML and some simple CSS. The first thing to do is to add the HTML code for your navigation:

```
<div id="navigation">
<h2>The Main navigation</h2>
<ul>
<li><a href=#>Home</a></li>
<li><a href=#>Store</a></li>
<li><a href=#>Blog</a></li>
<li><a href=#>Contact us</a>
</li>
</ul>
</div>
```

This is pretty self-explanatory, but if you look at the page now (10), the menu isn't looking too good—the list bullets are spilling over the edge of the container <div> and there is no padding between the text and the edge of the container.

The first thing you need to do to fix that is add a little padding to <h2> inside the #navigation <div>. This removes the bullets from our list and increases the line height in the list (11):

```
#navigation h2 {
padding-left: 10px;
padding-bottom: 10px;
}
#navigation li {
list-style: none;
line-height: 1.5em;
}
```

It's not too bad now, but it's a boring-looking menu and the menu items are touching the left side of the navigation div, which isn't too nice. The next chunk of CSS code is going to fix this (on the following page):

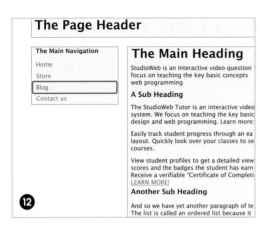

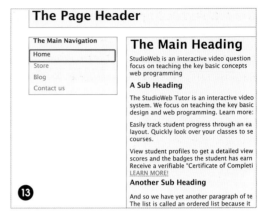

<a> tag set to display: inline.

```
#navigation a {

padding-left: 10px;

line-height: 2em;

text-decoration: none;

}

#navigation a:hover {

background-color: #FAFAD2;

display: block;

}
```

What this bit of CSS does first is target the <a> tags inside the #navigation <div>. The padding and line height changes that have been made are pretty self explanatory, while the next line— `text-decoration: none;—` removes the default hyperlink text underlines.

Next, the CSS pseudo class ":hover" is used to change the background color when the mouse hovers over a link.

Setting "display: block" means that the hover effect extends the entire width of the #navigation <div> (12).

If you set the display to "inline" instead (display: inline;) the <a> would have only taken up the width necessary for the text inside the <a> tag, as shown (13).

Nerd note

Block elements take up the full width of the space that is available. In this menu example, setting <a> to block meant that the <a> tag took up the full width of the #navigation <div>. This creates a nicer looking rollover or hover effect in the menu.

The problem with your static CSS layout

The page is now nicely structured, but there is one small problem: what happens if someone visits your site and their screen either does not have a high enough resolution to handle it, or their browser window is too narrow?

As shown below (14), when this happens the page gets cut off and and the user will have to manually scroll horizontally.

The solution to this problem is to use a liquid CSS layout.

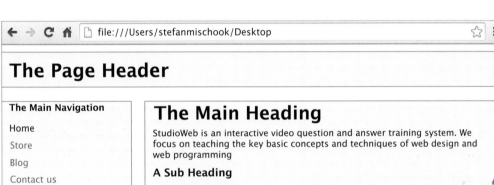

← → C ⌂ 🗋 file:///Users/stefanmischook/Desktop ☆ ≡

The Page Header

The Main Navigation

Home

Store

Blog

Contact us

The Main Heading

StudioWeb is an interactive video question and answer training system. We focus on teaching the key basic concepts and techniques of web design and web programming

A Sub Heading

The StudioWeb Tutor is an interactive video question and answer training system. We focus on teaching the key basic concepts and techniques of web design and web programming. Learn more:

Easily track student progress through an easy to read spreadsheet-like layout. Quickly look over your classes to see where students are in the courses.

View student profiles to get a detailed view of your student's progress: see scores and the badges the student has earned.
Receive a verifiable "Certificate of Completion" with each course you finish.
LEARN MORE!

Another Sub Heading

And so we have yet another paragraph of text that follows our ordered list. The list is called an ordered list because it has an order imposed upon it by the web browser - the list of items are numbered.

The Footer

Building a liquid CSS layout

The Page Header

Home
Store
Blog
Contact us

The Main Heading

StudioWeb is an interactive video question and answer training system. We focus on teaching the key basic concepts and techniques of web design and web programming

A Sub Heading

The StudioWeb Tutor is an interactive video question and answer training system. We focus on teaching the key basic concepts and techniques of web design and web programming. Learn more:

Easily track student progress through an easy to read spreadsheet-like layout. Quickly look over your classes to see where students are in the courses.

View student profiles to get a detailed view of your student's progress: see scores and the badges the student has earned.
Receive a verifiable "Certificate of Completion" with each course you finish. LEARN MORE!

Another Sub Heading

And so we have yet another paragraph of text that follows our odered list. The list is called an ordered list because it has an order imposed upon it by the web browser – the list of items are numbered.

StudioWeb is an interactive video question and answer training system. We focus on teaching the key basic concepts and techniques of web design and web programming

StudioWeb is an interactive video question and answer training system. We focus on teaching the key basic concepts and techniques of web design and web programming

StudioWeb is an interactive video question and answer training system. We focus on teaching the key basic concepts and techniques of web design and web programming

The Footer

Your sample site in "liquid" form.

To convert your static layout to a liquid layout is surprisingly easy. Liquid layouts are "in" these days, as it means your site will shrink and expand to meet the size of the web surfer's browser.

Generally speaking, you will probably want to go with liquid layouts. However, with a liquid design it can be harder to get the exact look that you want, as the design will be flexing according to the screen size.

Transforming a static page to a liquid layout

When you switch from a static to liquid layout everything about your page and CSS stays the same, with the exception of three key elements

1. You have to change your width values from pixels to percentages. Let's start with the #container <div> CSS (I'm just showing the width line here, as the rest of the CSS code remains the same):

```
#container {
width:90%;
}
```

The width has been changed from 960px to 90% of the browsers window. This means that as the window is resized, the layout will flex with it.

The liquid layout flowing to fit the size of the browser window.

2. The problem with setting the width to a percentage is that the browser window can be made so large that paragraphs of text run off too wide, or the browser window is so narrow that is squishes everything. You can avoid both of these things by adding two CSS attributes that limit the size of the page in pixels:

```
#container {
width:90%;
min-width: 400px;
max-width: 1250px;
}
```

Now, your page will expand and contract to stay at 90% of the window's width, but only down to 400px and up to 1250px.

When the page reaches one of these limits it will stop shrinking (at 400px) or expanding (at 1250px). Adding min-width and max-width essentially creates a liquid layout that has fixed layout behavior—the best of both worlds!

How wide and how narrow you set the limits of your pages depends on the content (if there are lots of images, for example) and on what your visitors are using to surf the web. For example, eight years ago the web traffic out there was very different from today, as nobody was using smartphones. The important thing is for you to clearly understand the principles and the basic techniques, so you can apply it on a case-by-case basis.

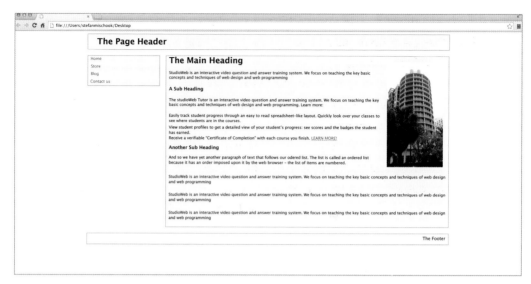

The page does not expand beyond the set max-width.

3. As with the #container <div>, you also need to change the #header, #footer, #centerDoc, and #navigation width sizes from pixels to percentages.

Because the #header and #footer have no other <div> at the left or right of them, you can set the width to 100%:

```
#header {
width:100%;
}
#footer {
width:100%;
}
```

However, the #navigation and #centerDoc divs are a bit trickier, as they sit beside each other (horizontally). This mean you have to calculate the percentage of the page that each element occupies. I did a bit of tinkering and testing and came up with these values:

```
#centerDoc {
width: 78%;
margin-left: 1%;
}
#navigation {
width: 20%;
}
```

Again, I have removed all the other CSS code from these examples, as it is no different to the fixed layout.

Note that you don't need to set margin-top and margin-bottom to percentages, as there is plenty of space vertically (with scrolling). You only need to concern yourself with the page's horizontal display.

Liquid font sizes

In both the static and liquid layouts, you have been setting font sizes using ems rather than pixels, although you could do either:

```
body {font-size: 12px}
```
or
```
body {font-size: 1em}
```

The main difference is that font sizes that are pixel based are fixed, while font sizes that are em based are liquid. Pixel-based sizes are easy to understand, but ems will take another sentence or two.

Setting fonts to an em size allows users to resize the text in the browser menu and is the preferred way for web designers to set font sizes. 1 em is equal to the current (pixel-based) font size, which means that 1.2 em would be a font size that is 20% larger. So, if the default font size for the browser is 10px, then:

```
1em = 10px
1.2em = 12px
```

The default text size in most browsers is 16 pixels (I just used 10px in this example to keep the math simple). However, you might want to change the default size of the page's font using the universal selector, just as you did with your margins and padding:

```
* {
margin: 0; padding: 0;
font-size: 12px;
}
```

Then, having set a new "default" size, you can use ems to size the fonts in the rest of the CSS.

Time for a break—this chapter is done!

Whoa! This has been a big chapter with a lot to take in—it was tough writing it, so I imagine you got a headache reading it! Now is a good time to take a break, but when you are ready come back and try out the examples. Change things as you go through and see how it works, or if you can break it! Watching things break can be very educational—or at least that's what I tell myself every time a break a glass!

CHAPTER 9

Building & Styling HTML Tables

You've covered a lot of the tricky details and nerd-theories in the first half of the book—good work! Now you can build from that base and explore a bunch of things that add pizazz and dazzle to a website.

Everyone knows that a toolbox can be a lot of fun—at least that's what my father keeps telling me. Anyway, our Toolbox is definitely one of those fun boxes, so let's dive in!

I decided to start with the least exciting thing in the Toolbox—HTML tables—because I don't want to shock you with too much excitement. Nonetheless, HTML tables are still kind of cool, and they actually have an interesting history in the world of web design—they're the fallen stars of web design! Once central to the process of building websites, HTML tables are now only supporting (although still important) actors on the web design stage.

HTML tables are designed to present tabular data (think spreadsheets) so they can be used to display price lists, schedules, and similar items. In this chapter you will learn how to use HTML tables to create a spreadsheet-like structure in your web pages, and at the same time you will explore CSS further.

Tables are flexible and can also hold images (using the image tag, or CSS of course), video, or any other HTML that you want. Generally speaking, though, you want to limit what you put in tables to mostly text and—occasionally—images.

Back in the old days of web design, when the dinosaurs walked the earth and I had really, really long hair (about 1997), people used tables to lay out entire web pages. This was because there was no other way to do it—CSS was just a figment of a nerd's imagination.

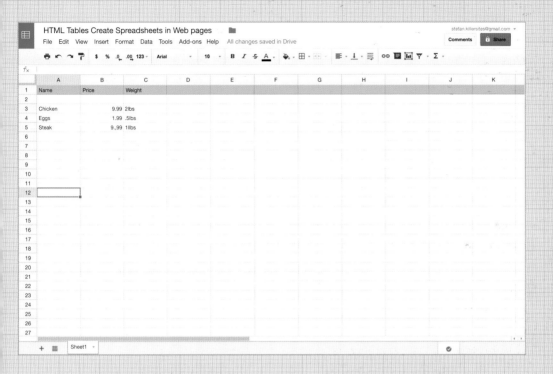

In fact, my predecessor at killersites.com (David Siegel) wrote a famous book on how to use HTML tables combined with transparent gifs to lay out web pages. Thankfully he had the foresight to say that using tables was only a bandaid solution until CSS could come of age.

Anyway, those days are now long gone, and I only mention it in case you run into an ancient website that uses tables—you will at least know what's going on before you strip all the ugly table code away!

HTML tables allow you to create spreadsheet like structures in your websites. Pictured here is Google's fully functional spreadsheet app that is actually created with the help of HTML tables.

To be clear: tables are a great way of presenting tabular data (as we are about to do), but they should *never* be used to lay out entire pages—this is a 1990s web design technique and we shall not speak of it again! To do so would be very close to heresy!

Building an HTML table

Let's start by building a very basic HTML table. For this example I will omit all the other HTML from the page to save paper (besides, I think you know how to build a basic web page by now!). The table code looks like this:

```
<table>
<tr><td></td><td></td></tr>
<tr><td></td><td></td></tr>
</table>
```

This code creates the simplest table you can get. The opening and closing <table> tags are self explanatory, but what about the new tags you have used?

The <tr> tag is short for "table row," so each pair of <tr> tags creates a single row in your table. In this example, you have created two rows (1).

The <td> tag is short for "table data," which creates a vertical column. In this example you have two columns, as there are two sets of <td> tags (2).

If you take a closer look at the code in images 1 and 2, you will see that I inserted some data into the table:

```
<td>Apples</td><td>$1.99</td>
<td>Bananas</td><td>$1.25</td>
```

```
html-tables-01.html  x
1  <!doctype html>
2  <html lang="en-US">
3  <head>
4      <meta charset="utf-8">
5      <title>HTML Tables</title>
6  </head>
7  <body>
8
9  <table>
10 <table>
11     <tr><td>Apples </td><td>$1.99</td></tr>     (row1)
12     <tr><td>Bananas </td><td>$1.25</td></tr>    (row2)
13
14 </table>
15
16
17 </body>
18 </html>
```

```
html-tables-01.html  x
1  <!doctype html>
2  <html lang="en-US">
3  <head>
4      <meta charset="utf-8">
5      <title>HTML Tables</title>
6  </head>
7  <body>
8
9              (column 1)    (column 2)
10 <table>
11     <tr><td>Apples </td> <td>$1.99</td></tr>
12     <tr><td>Bananas </td><td>$1.25</td></tr>
13 </table>
14
15
16
17 </body>
18 </html>
```

At the moment, your table doesn't really look like a table (3), because you can't see any of the borders. So, let's add a border with CSS, so you can see what you are doing. Add this in the <head> of you HTML page:

```
<style type="text/css">
table, td, th {border:1px solid
black;}
</style>
```

This CSS code adds a one pixel black border to your table and table cells. It doesn't look great right now, but you can at least see the table (4). We will make it look good soon.

Sub tags

Sub tags must exist inside their parent tags. For example, <tr> is a sub tag of <table>, so you can never use <tr> outside of <table>. At the same time, <td> is a sub tag of <tr>, so you can never use <td> outside of <tr>. In earlier chapters you saw a similar thing with <li>, which is a sub tag of <ol>.

What are table cells?

Table "cells" can be either <td>s or <th>s. <td> is short for "table data;" <th> is short for "table header."

These are just two different types of table cells, although in everyday web design, most people will just refer to them both as table cells.

More table sub tags

Tables are one of those tags in HTML that have many sub tags. So far you've seen <tr> and <td>, but what if you want to create a row that acts as your table header (5)? Let's say that you want to title your two columns:

```
<table>
<tr><th>Fruit</th><th>Price
</th></tr>
<tr><td>Apples:</td><td>$1.99
</td></tr>
<tr><td>Bananas</td><td>$1.25
</td></tr>
</table>
```

5

Here, the <th> tag is short for "table header." By default, web browsers will make <th> text bold and align it centrally. However, as you will see shortly, you can override this default using CSS.

The table <caption> tag

You can add a caption to your table using the <caption> tag (6):

```
<table>
<caption>My Fruit Price list
</caption>
<tr><th>Fruit</th><th>Price
</th></tr>
<tr><td>Apples</td><td>$1.99
</td></tr>
<tr><td>Bananas</td><td>$1.25
</td></tr>
</table>
```

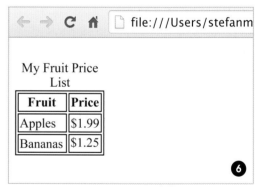

6

Our table looks terrible, so that's enough about HTML tags for now—let's see how CSS can be used to make the table look halfway presentable.

CSS table styling

As with the HTML tags, you could apply our CSS directly inline (in the tags themselves). As you know, this is typically the wrong thing to do, and for a live site it is better to have all your CSS in an external style sheet. However, for the sake of this walkthrough, since this is only a one-page website, I will be placing them in the <head> section of our web page.

Controlling the table width

The first thing to do is give this table some breathing room—it's too squished up at the moment! For this first code snippet I'm showing all the tags found in the <head> section, so you know where you are. However, as you continue to style your table, I will just show the CSS code. Let's start by adding this CSS code:

```
<head>
<meta charset="utf-8">
<title>HTML Tables</title>
<style type="text/css">
table, td, th {border:1px solid
black;}
table {width: 50%;}   /* NEW CSS
CODE*/
</style>
</head>
```

The new line of CSS code indicated above basically gives the table a width of 50% of the page width. You could also set it to pixels, or even better, use the max-width property you learned about in Chapter 8 to limit the table's width (7):

```
table {
width: 50%;
max-width: 500px;
}
```

The table doesn't look bad so far, but it still looks a little tight for my taste.

My Fruit Price List	
Fruit	**Price**
Apples	$1.99
Bananas	$1.25

7

Default alignments

One thing that increasing your table width will reveal is that by default, text is aligned left in <td> cells and centered in <th> cells.

Adjusting the appearance of the table using CSS

Adding some padding to the cells will space things out a bit (8):

```
<style type="text/css">
table, td, th {border:1px solid
black;}
table {width: 50%;}
td, th {padding: 10px;}
</style>
```

As you can see, it's looking better, but there is still work to do. Let's center-align the <td> text, give the <caption> a pink background color, increase the font size, and add some padding:

```
td {text-align: center;}
caption {font-size: 2em; padding:
10px; background-color: #FFA5A7;}
```

This is much better, but I reckon the font color should be gray (9):

```
caption {font-size: 2em; padding:
10px; background-color: #FFA5A7;
color: gray}
```

Finally, as a finishing touch let's center the table horizontally (10). That's easy to achieve—you can just use "margin: auto;" If you put all your CSS code together it should look like this:

```
<style type="text/css">
table, td, th {border:1px solid
black;}
table {width: 50%;}
td, th {padding: 10px;}
td {text-align: center;}
caption {font-size: 2em; padding:
10px; background-color: #FFA5A7;
color: gray}
table {margin: auto;}
</style>
```

My Fruit Price List

Fruit	Price
Apples	$1.99
Bananas	$1.25

(10)

My Fruit Price List

Fruit	Price	Quantity
Apples	$1.99	25
Bananas	$1.85	30
Grapes	$1.67	100
Pineapple	$2.25	2
Blue Berries	$1.25	50
Black Rhino	-	-

(11)

Combining table columns and rows

Sometimes you will need to combine rows and columns to better present your data. It will be easier to demonstrate this if you add a few more rows and one more column to your table:

```
<table>
<caption>My Fruit Price List
</caption>
<tr><th>Fruit</th><th>Price
</th><th>Quantity</th></tr>
<tr><td>Apples </td><td>$1.99
</td><td>25</td></tr>
<tr><td>Bananas</td><td>$1.25
</td><td>50</td></tr>
<tr><td>Grapes</td><td>$1.25
</td><td>50</td></tr>
<tr><td>Pineapple</td><td>$1.25
</td><td>50</td></tr>
<tr><td>Blue Berries<td>
<td>$1.25</td><td>50</td></tr>
<tr><td>Black Rhino</td><td>
no stock</td></tr>
</table>
```

As you can see, there's now a "Quantity" column and a few more rows with new fruit and a black rhino (11). As black rhinos are exceptionally rare, there's no price or quantity for this item, so it makes sense to combine these two columns on this row. To do that, you will use the "colspan" attribute on the second <td> so that it spans not one, but two columns:

```
<tr><td>Black Rhino</td>
<td colspan="2">-</td><td>-</td>
</tr>
```

Now, there's a problem with the code. Check out how the table looks (12)—you need to remove one set of <td> tags from that bottom row. Why? Well, let's read the code in another way:

```
<td colspan="2">
```

This basically says that this particular <td> spans two columns instead of the usual one column, so it takes up two spaces instead of one. However, you need to remove the <td> tag pair at the end of the row, because although its spot is being used up by your column-spanning <td>, the third column doesn't just disappear—it moves along. So you need to change your code (13):

```
<tr><td>Black Rhino</td><td
colspan="2">-</td></tr>
```

"Rowspan" works in the same way as colspan, but it combines rows, rather than columns, as demonstrated by this simple table (14):

```
<table>
<caption>Contact List</caption>
<tr><th>First Name:</th>
<td>Steve Jobs</td></tr>
<tr>
<th rowspan="2">Telephone:</th>
<td>555 77 854</td>
</tr><tr>
<td>666 77 855</td>
</tr>
</table>
```

164

If you find it a little harder to see how the code relates to the result on the page, remember that with colspan you had to drop one set of <td> tags to make room for the expanded column. There's a similar thing happening here—in the last row, the second cell (a <td>) has been removed to make space for the row on top.

So, although you have three <tr> tag sets (three rows), in the first column you are only displaying two rows. You may have to play around with it for it to make sense.

Styling specific table columns with the CSS3 :nth-child() selector

I think the best way to open this topic is by saying: "What the heck is an :nth-child() selector!"

In a nutshell: this is some super-cool CSS pseudo-code that allows you to easily target elements in your pages that otherwise would be a major pain. When I first saw the :nth-child() selector, I thought I'd died and gone to nerd heaven!

The CSS3 :nth-child() selector is part of the latest and greatest version of CSS— CSS3. No worries though, because all the major browsers support it, so you can use it confidently in your websites.

In this particular example, I very much think it's best to start with the results at the outset, and then we can deconstruct all the specifics about how this code actually works. So start by checking out the screenshot (15).

I was able to turn the last column light pink and adjust the width of the column with this CSS code:

```
td:nth-child(3) {
background: #FFCCCC;
width: 15%;
}
```

My Fruit Price List		
Fruit	**Price**	**Quantity**
Apples	$1.99	25
Bananas	$1.85	30
Grapes	$1.67	100
Pineapple	$2.25	2
Blue Berries	$1.25	50

The :nth-child() selector allows you to select sub tags or child tags. So, in this case it says select any <td> tags on the page that are the third child of its parent tag (the parent here is the <tr> tag).

Now, if the code had been: th:nth-child(3), you would be selecting any <th> tag, rather than any <td> tag. This would be the result (16):

My Fruit Price List

Fruit	Price	Quantity
Apples	$1.99	25
Bananas	$1.85	30
Grapes	$1.67	100
Pineapple	$2.25	2
Blue Berries	$1.25	50

16

If you look at it from another angle, you can see that the top row of the 3rd column was not given a background color of pink in the first example (15) because the top row uses <th> and not <td>— your CSS said to target the <td> tags.

Zebra striping your table with :nth-child() The :nth-child() is full of surprises. For example, you can use it to target even or odd numbered occurrences of a tag, which is cool for coloring table rows. Here is the code:

```
tr:nth-child(even) {
background: #FFCCCC;
width: 15%
}
```

This code is saying "target any <tr> if it is the even child of its parent, and then change the background color to #FFCCCC." Check out the screenshot to see the effect it has (17).

My Fruit Price List

Fruit	Price	Quantity
Apples	$1.99	25
Bananas	$1.85	30
Grapes	$1.67	100
Pineapple	$2.25	2
Blue Berries	$1.25	50

17

In this example, the code doesn't give the first row a background color because "1" is not an even number. In other words, it's only styling rows 2, 4, and 6.

You can also change the CSS so it targets the odd child tags instead:

```
tr:nth-child(odd) {
background: #FFCCCC;
width: 15%
}
```

Old school table formatting vs. CSS

Older versions of HTML supplied a bunch of tag attributes in <table> tags that were used to style or format tables. These formatting attributes have been replaced by CSS and should now never be used. That said, you may run into them, so it's worth seeing what they look like. For example, this is an old school <table> attribute that adds a border to a table:

```
<table border="1">
...
</table>
```

To be clear, this is not inline CSS, it is the HTML "border" attribute. Inline CSS always starts with the style attribute, so it would be:

```
<table style="width:100%">
...
</table>
```

Global HTML attributes

The HTML style attribute (style=" ") is an example of a "global" HTML attribute, which means the attribute can be used with any HTML tag. This makes sense because we want to be able to apply CSS universally.

Some last thoughts about web design (for this chapter)

As you probably noticed, web design has grown up in a messy way, with lots of conflicts over how HTML and CSS should work. This has led to many revisions and changes to specifications, which in turn have created compatibility issues between browsers.

Fortunately, all of these battles have pretty much been resolved and things are now fairly well established in the web-design world.

CHAPTER 10

Forms, CSS & Images

HTML forms are used to collect information from users. They are super important in web design because almost every website will need to do this.

Forms are also one of the more complex HTML tags, as there are several important attributes that need to be understood, as well as many sub tags.

After an initial look at HTML forms, we will dive back into CSS, looking at how it can be used to insert images into web pages. Then you will learn how to make your CSS more compact.

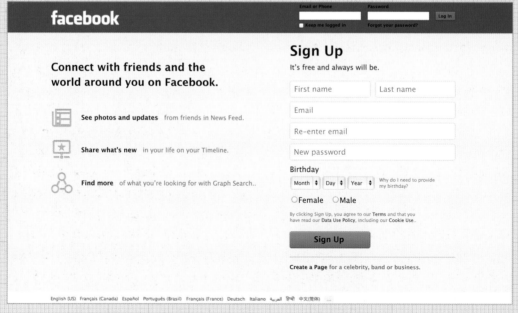

The Facebook signup form is one of the most famous forms in the world.

HTML forms

When the web was first invented it was just an elegant system of exchanging information with the world using a simple page paradigm. Yet there was a problem with simple web pages—there was no way to gather information from people who were visiting a web site. To solve this problem, some smart people came up with HTML forms.

What is an HTML form?

An HTML form is made up of a bunch of HTML tags that allow people visiting websites to enter information (or select information from a list) that is transmitted to the server for processing. You use forms every day—when you log into Facebook, Twitter, or your bank account online, for example, you are using forms.

To make an HTML form, you start with the mother of all form tags:

```
<form action="myFormScript.php "
method="post" >
</form>
```

This set of opening and closing form tags defines the region of the form: any form tags inserted between these two tags are considered (by the browser) to be part of the same form.

The "action" attribute tells the browser where to send the information that is entered into the form, while the "method" attribute tells the browser *how* to send that information (more on that later). You could have multiple forms on the same page—for example:

```
<body>
<h3>This is the first log in
form.</h3>
<form action="myFormScript.php"
method="post" id="loginForm">
</form>
<h3>This is another form—amazing!
</h3>
<form action="anotherFormProcessor.
php " method="post" id="last-
passwordForm">
</form>
</body>
```

You'll notice that I've given each form an ID here. This isn't required to make the forms work, but it makes it as clear as possible that although these two forms are on the same page, they have nothing to do with each other. Another reason I give each form its own ID is to show that you can then use CSS to style each of them, just like any other tag or element on the page.

What you should take away is that data collected in one form on a page will have nothing to do with the data collected in another form, on the same page. Each form is its own container for collecting information from people.

It might help to think of forms as being boxes; each box holds whatever information you put into it, and then you can move the boxes wherever you like, independent of each other.

The limits of HTML forms

Forms do only two things. First, they provide a place for people to enter in information, and second, forms can send or submit that information to an app. The app can then process the information held in the form.

So if you create an HTML form in a web page, don't think that the information will be automatically processed for you—it won't. To process the information held in a form, you need a web developer or programmer to write the app that can do this. Typically this is done with languages like PHP, Java, or Ruby, and there are many others.

Forms & HTML5 Web Storage

With the advent of HTML5, forms can also be used to capture information to be stored right on the user's computer. This works thanks to a new mechanism called "Web Storage" that lets programmers save information without needing a server and a server-side programming language such as PHP.

Forms can't do it alone though— you still need programming skills and that's where (once again) JavaScript comes into the picture.

Web storage is not something to get into in a beginners' book, but it is still useful to know your options.

Be careful while creating forms

Be sure not to nest your forms! If you do, you will be asking for trouble.

Form sub tags

To actually collect any user data to start with, the user needs a place to type in information or select the information from. This is where form sub tags come in. There are a lot of these, but here are the most important ones:

```
<input>
<textarea>
<select>
```

To put this into practice, let's build a simple form (1). Open up your text editor or code editor and create a simple HTML page. In the <body> add these tags:

```
<form action="myFormScript.php"
method="post">
Name: <input type="text">
Password: <input type="password">
<input type="submit" >
</form>
```

The <input> tag

There are two interesting things about <input> tags. First, they are one of the few HTML tags that stand alone—they do not have a closing tag. Second, <input> tags can change a lot depending on the value you give to the "type" attribute.

Here, for example, you have used three <input> tags with three different type attribute values: text, password, and submit. Typing "text" creates a text box; "password" gives a text box that hides the characters; and "submit" creates the submit button that sends the form to its target. (A form's target is set using the <form> tag's "action" attribute: in this case, the form is set to send its information to myFormScript.php.)

| Name: | stefan | Password: | •••••••• | Submit |

1

Text box terminology

Text boxes, input type text, and text field are all different names for the same thing. Depending on the web designer you speak to, you may hear any one of these.

As the <input> tag is an inline tag, the different form elements just spread out across the page. If you want to stack the text boxes, you can use CSS to turn them into block tags (2):

```
<style type="text/css">
input {
display: block;
margin-top: 0em;
}
</style>
```

The form with "display: block" applied.

Alternatively, you could use <br> tags to add line-breaks after each <input> box (3):

```
Name: <input type="text"> <br>
Password: <input type="password">
<br>
```

The form with <br> tags in place.

It is worth noting that these options are not exactly the same. Using a <br>, the text stays on the same line, whereas transforming the <input> tags to block level tags forces the text onto another line. Neither method is better than the other—it's project dependent. Although I would lean toward using CSS, since you will have less HTML in your code (no <br> tags, that is).

Controlling the size in input boxes

The <input> tag has many attributes; one of the most important of these is the size attribute, which controls how much room the text box displays:

```
Name: <input type="text" size="50">
<br>
Password: <input type="password"
size="50"> <br>
```

For both the of the input boxes above, the size is set to 50 (4), which means browsers will expand the <input> tags to display 50 characters. As with all HTML tags, the browsers have default values for text boxes, so it's a good idea to set your own size.

The form with text inputs set to 50.

Identifying the input tags with the "name" attribute

Let's take a look at one last attribute that <input> tags have: name. Here's the relevant code:

```
Name: <input type="text" size="50"
name="user-name"> <br>
Password: <input type="password"
size="50" name="pwd"> <br>
```

The "name" attribute is very important for two reasons. First, if you submit a form and you don't supply the name attribute to an <input> tag, the information collected by that tag will not be sent to the server for processing. Second, the server-side apps that process forms need the name attribute to be able to process the form to begin with.

When giving a value to a name attribute, you should follow the web design naming conventions: don't use funny symbols and don't add spaces between words (use dashes or underscores instead).

Creating check boxes with <input> tags

Now let's create a check box using this code (5):

```
<input type="checkbox"
name="vehicle" value="Ford"> I have
a Ford<br>
<input type="checkbox"
name="vehicle" value="Audi"> I have
an Audi<br>
```

This input type can be confusing—I still get mixed up from time to time! With the checkbox input type, all checkboxes that have the same name (in our case it is "vehicle") are grouped together as a logical unit—they are considered part of the same input.

When this gets sent to the server for processing, all the checkbox <input> tags with a name of "vehicle" will be grouped together by the server app that is processing the form. If this is unclear,

don't worry—it will only come up when you have to work with a programmer or decide to get into web app creation.

The <textarea> tag

The <textarea> tag creates a multi-line text box. Some nerds might call it a "multi-line text input control."

The <textarea> tag has two attributes: rows and cols. These attributes allow to set how many rows and columns the text box has. Check out the code:

```
<textarea rows="5" cols="50">
Man, I can put a lot of text in
here! This form element is huge!
</textarea>
```

The number attached to the rows and cols in the code refers to the number of characters. So, in this example, the text box allows 5 rows of text (characters) and 50 columns of text (characters).

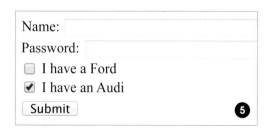

The form with input type="checkbox."

The form with the <textarea> tag.

The <select> tag

The <select> tag creates what is sometimes called a dropdown list—when you see it in action, you will know why:

```
<select name="car-type">
<option value="ford">Ford</option>
<option value="fiat">Fiat</option>
<option value="merc">Mercedes</option>
<option value="audi">Audi</option>
</select>
```

You will notice that <select> has a sub tag, <option>. Each <option> tag allows you to specify an option in the list. So, if someone were to select the third option—Mercedes—and then submit the form, the server would get this information:

```
car-type=merc
```

Remember that when sending information to the server, the form sends the value, not what is displayed to the user. So, although "Mercedes" is displayed to the user, "merc" is the value that is sent.

A last word on forms

I've only scratched the surface in terms of all the form tags and options you have to choose from—the <input> tag's type attribute has 24 values alone!

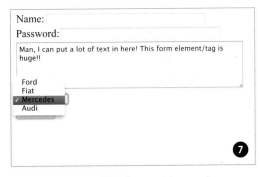

The form with a <select> tag.

However, you have covered the most commonly used tags, and more importantly, you now know the basic principles of forms. Learning more should now be fairly easy.

There are many places to learn more about forms on the web; a great place for people who already understand the basics is at the W3C: http://www.w3schools.com/html/html_forms.asp.

If you find videos helpful, check out webmentor.org where I have many videos on forms (and a bunch of other web-design related topics). You will also find videos made specifically to complement this book on the accompanying website.

Using CSS to insert images

Besides using the <img> tag, you also have the option to insert images into your web pages using CSS. Basically, you do this by making an image the background of a block level tag, such as a <div> or even the <body>. For example:

```
body {
background-image:url("miami-top-
banner-gradient.png");
background-position:center top;
background-repeat: no-repeat;
}
```

The first property (background-image:url,) is pretty self explanatory—you just set the path to the image you want to use as a background. The next two probably need a little explaining:

```
background-position:center top
```

This code positions the image within the tag, in this case the <body> tag. Here are the available positioning options:

```
left top
left center
left bottom
```

What do I mean by "path?"

Think of an actual path or trail. It is just a way of describing where in the file system, or where in the folders, a file is situated. The file could be an image, a CSS page, an HTML page—anything. So if you have the image "fish.png" inside a folder called "images," the path to that folder would be: images/fish.png.

```
right top
right center
right bottom
center top
center center
center bottom
```

The last property—background-repeat: no-repeat;—allows you to control whether the image is tiled or not. The options are:

```
background-repeat: no-repeat;
background-repeat: repeat-x;
background-repeat: repeat-y;
```

Let's look at a practical example that starts with a simple web page:

```
<body>
<div>
<p>…</p>
</div>
</body>
```

To save space, I've replaced all the text in the paragraph with three dots (…). Here's the CSS that goes with the page:

```
<style type="text/css">
div {
font-size: 1.2em;
width: 50%;
margin: auto;
padding: 2%;
padding-top: .1%;
border-width: 1px;
border-style: solid;
border-color: #708DB5;
color: #FFF;
background-color: #708DB5;
}
p::first-letter {
font-size: 3em;
color: #FFF;
}
</style>
```

Most of this CSS you've seen before, but note that I centered the <div> horizontally using "margin: auto;" I also added some padding to give the text some space; and I used the "::first-letter" CSS pseudo selector on the <p> tag to target the first letter in a tag. In this example, I increased the first letter in the <p> to 3em, so it is three times the size of the page's standard font size (1).

Lorem ipsum dolor sit amet, consectetur adipiscing elit. Maecenas id aliquam libero. Donec ac sapien erat. Duis pellentesque nulla id sem blandit faucibus et at lectus. Maecenas bibendum risus sit amet eleifend fringilla. Curabitur placerat lorem in ligula luctus convallis. In tristique sem nisl, a gravida leo facilisis nec. In mattis lectus vel quam bibendum rutrum. Vestibulum tempus lacus ut lectus eleifend, nec varius orci varius. Nunc felis ex, tincidunt vitae rhoncus non, blandit vel ipsum. In at tincidunt ex, vel faucibus tellus. Sed ultrices tincidunt risus non feugiat. Aenean porttitor non sapien a luctus. Suspendisse ac consequat nulla. Sed ac vulputate est.

A <p> with the pseudo class ::first-letter applied.

The image applied to bottom right.

What we have done so far looks OK, but now let's add a background image using this code inside the div CSS selector (2):

```
background-image: url("small-image.
png");
background-position: right bottom;
background-repeat: no-repeat;
```

Not bad. However, the text overlaps the background image. You will fix that in a minute, but before you do, let's see what happens if you comment out the "no-repeat":

```
background-image: url("small-image.
png");
background-position: right bottom;
/*background-repeat: no-repeat;*/
```

If you remember, in CSS, when you surround code or text with "/* code or text here*/" the browser ignores it. So when you comment out the "no-repeat" line you essentially delete it from the effect on the page.

As you can see, the background image is now tiled on the page (3). This can be useful with, say, a pattern that you want to use as a background, but it definitely doesn't work here!

Let's make it work by changing the position to the top and adding a little more top padding to push the text down, and give the image room (4):

```
background-position: right top;
padding-top: 7%;
```

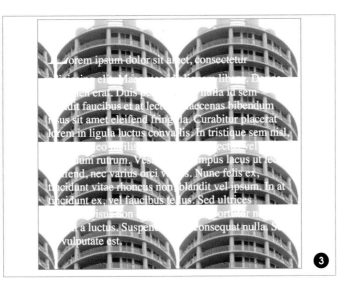

"No-repeat" is commented out. So the image repeats!

Image position top right.

Let's finish looking at CSS and background images by checking out a practical example—using CSS to insert a nice-looking top banner. I've gone back to the template from Chapter 8 and made a few modifications to the code (I've removed the margins between the structural <div> tags, changed the colors, and removed the <div> outlines). The result is the web page shown below (5).

This isn't bad, but let's add a header background image using CSS (6):

```
#header {
height: 107px;
margin-bottom: 20px;
background-image:url("miami-top-
banner-gradient.png");
background-repeat: no-repeat;
background-position:center top;
}
```

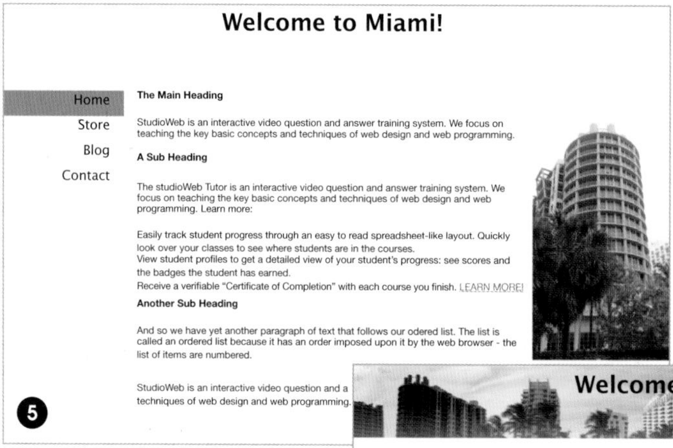

Where's the header image?!

Better with the header, but it needs work.

This is better, but I know that the header image is 207 pixels tall, so if you want to see it all you will need to increase the #header height to 207 pixels. While you're at it, move the <h1> tag with the "Welcome to Miami" text to the right with a float (7):

```
#header h1 {
padding: 10px;
float: right;
color: #000;}
```

There are other ways you can position background images that I won't cover here (we have many other things to cover!), but I will be creating free videos for you guys that expand on this subject. Check out the book's website for details.

Ahh ... now that's a nice header!

Making CSS more compact

Let's finish off this chapter with a few easy CSS techniques that will make writing CSS more compact (and easier to write!).

Margin and padding

```
div {
margin-top: 1em;
margin-right: 1.5em;
margin-bottom: 2em;
margin-left: 2.5em;
}
```

We can combine all these rules like this:

```
div {
margin: 1em 1.5em 2em 2.5em;
}
```

As you saw in Chapter 4, if you combine the CSS on one line, the order has to be: top, right, bottom, left. It is exactly the same for padding as it is for margins.

Fonts

There is a compact method for fonts too:

```
body {
font-size: 1.5em;
line-height: 200%;
font-weight: bold;
font-style: italic;
```

```
font-family: Georgia, "Times New
Roman", serif;
}
```

Can be condensed into:

```
body {
font: 1.5em/200% bold italic
Georgia,"Times New Roman", serif;
}
```

Note that with fonts, the order of the values has to be the same as it is in this example.

Background images

Now the compact CSS for background images:

```
div {
background-color: #000;
background-image: url(image.gif);
background-repeat: no-repeat;
background-position: top left;
}
```

Becomes:

```
div {
background: #000 url(image.gif) no-
repeat top left;
}
```

List

Compacting a CSS list:

```css
ul {
list-style-type: circle;
list-style-position: inside;
list-style-image: url(bullet.gif);
}
```

Becomes:

```css
ul {
list-style: circle inside
url(bullet.gif);
}
```

Borders

```css
p {
border-width: 1px;
border-style: solid;
border-color: red;
}
```

Becomes:

```css
p {
border: 1px solid red;
}
```

When combining the CSS on one line for background images, lists, and borders you don't have to worry about the order of the values.

Suggested chapter exercises

If you haven't already, I would suggest trying out some of the CSS code found in this chapter.

Create a new page with a few paragraphs of text and then use CSS to add a background image. Finally, try using some of the compact CSS code covered on tehse pages. The more code you write, the faster you will learn.

Some final words on this chapter

When you look at forms and how they fit into the web design mix, you start to see how web designers need to understand the web app creation process—at least on a fundamental level.

In modern web design, web designers are often working on websites that have some sort of functionality, which blurs the lines between a classic website and web apps. This is the reason why I've been teaching you a little bit about programming and programming languages.

CHAPTER 11

HTML5 & CSS3

We've been touching on HTML5 throughout the book, starting with the HTML5 doctype and a few other minor details. In this chapter, you are going to focus more clearly on what HTML5 and CSS3 bring to the web design table.

This includes things like embedding video and audio using HTML5, a new set of HTML5 semantic tags that give much more meaning to your pages, and CSS3 effects such as box-shadows.

As I mentioned earlier in the book, HTML5 is the latest and greatest version of HTML, representing a major shift in the web design world. In the not too distant past, XHTML was dominant. Although HTML5 looks very similar, it has a totally different foundation and a very different philosophy behind it.

XHTML was developed with the mindset that web browsers and websites should bend and contort to XHTML specification. The whole web design community got silly stupid doing this and it ended up causing a huge amount of headaches.

On the other hand, HTML5 was put together by rebel nerds who thought that the specification for building websites should be pragmatic and respect how pages had been built in the past. The HTML5 guys did not want to break half the web in the way that XHTML did.

Obviously there's much more to it than that, but what you should appreciate is that XHTML was rigid and very academic whereas HTML5 is sympathetic to the way in which people build websites. HTML5 won the war because it is always better to be practical than dogmatic!

HTML5 & CSS3

The new version of CSS is CSS3, which is typically lumped together with HTML5 because both are part of the same seismic shift in the web design process. However, even though HTML5 and CSS3 have an

Twitter makes use of HTML5 full-screen images—a technique you'll learn in this chapter.
Ref: https://twitter.com

An example of how HTML5 and CSS3 can create a great-looking site—in this example, images animate and flow as the user scrolls.
Ref: http://risotteriamelottinyc.com

official specification, it is not totally supported by browsers, which means a lot of things just don't work yet. This inconsistent compatibility among web browsers is normal in the web world, and the good thing is that many of the techniques do work in the vast majority of web browsers.

That said, you may have to compensate for dinosaur companies who are using typewriters and web browsers from the 1960s. Check out the book's website for more tips on how to deal with this.

Browser support & HTML5

The CSS3 and HTML5 that you are going to cover in this book will work in about 96–99% of browsers being used today. For me, that is an acceptable percentage.

The browser that is causing all the problems is Internet Explorer 8 (IE8) and to a lesser extent IE9. The good thing is that IE8 has less than 4% of the market share and this figure is dropping: by the time you read this, it will certainly be lower still.

HTML5 represents a seismic shift in the web design world, allowing designers to incorporate the latest multimedia technology and vastly improving cross-browser compatibility.

Caniuse.com is a good place to check browser compatibility.

Checking to see which browsers support web fonts.

Dealing with old browsers

One of the hassles that web designers have had to deal with since the early days of the web is older web browsers that don't work well with the latest code standards—the current versions of HTML and CSS. For many years even basic CSS didn't work at all!

This still happens a bit today, but as it is marginal I don't think it's worth cluttering up these pages with "fixes" for old browsers that have less than 4% of the market share. I will teach you one quick fix when we get into the new HTML5 structural tags, but I won't get into the other stuff—sometimes in life and in tech, you have to leave the old behind so you can move forward!

Checking browser support

Whole books have been written on HTML5 and CSS3, so I will be covering just the most important (and coolest!) things that will work in that aforementioned 96%+ of web browsers.

However, things do (and will continue to) change as the new HTML5 and CSS3 become widely supported by the various web browsers. This makes it a good idea to check from time to time what you can use in your websites.

There are a few places you can go for this information—http://caniuse.com is a good one, and an easy way to check out browser compatibility. For example, under the CSS heading, you will find a link to

@font-face web fonts. This is CSS3 that allows you to import fonts into your web pages. If you click on the link on the website you will be shown a chart that shows which browsers support @font-face, and which ones do not—if the box is green, you are good to go. (The @font-face rule means that web designers don't have to use one of the old "web-safe" fonts, which I list over the page. As so often, there is a complex way and an easy way to use @font-face; since Google provides a free service that makes using @font-face easy, we'll learn about that method, rather than the complex one, in the pages coming up.)

Thanks to the use of HTML5 and CSS3, subtle animations bring this website to life.
Ref: http://www.bluhomes.com

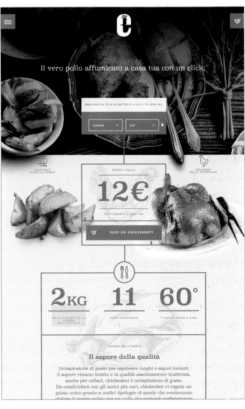

A striking-looking website for a very simple concept—thanks to the new technologies.
Ref: http://www.chickenbot.it

CSS & fonts

Fonts go a long way to setting the mood of a web page, so are super important in design. You wouldn't, for example, use the sort of gothic, vampire-like monster font shown below for the website of a baby birthday cake business!

GOTHIC

You've already been using fonts in the pages you've worked through, but I haven't got into details about how fonts work in web design. So let's start with a few basics.

When you set font types in your CSS, you are limited to fonts that you can expect the person viewing your website to already have installed on their own computer. Because of this limitation, you usually have to stick to fonts that come built into Windows and Mac operating systems, which isn't many!

However, when you set font types in CSS, you can start with a specific font names, but also add the more general font family. If the specific font isn't on the visitor's computer, then they can at least use a font from the same family, so the page design (hopefully) remains similar. For example:

```
p {
font-family: "Times New Roman",
Times, serif;
}
```

In this code, the font is set to Times New Roman, but if the user doesn't have that font installed, the font family "Times" is specified as an alternative (so a font from this family would be used instead). As a last resort, if the viewer doesn't have a font from the Times family, a "serif" font is a third option.

Web-safe fonts
These fonts you can be safely used in your web pages as they are typically installed on Windows, Mac, and Unix-based computers:

Arial
Courier/Courier New
Helvetica
Times/Times New Roman

In addition, these fonts work on most Windows and Mac computers:

Not free, but a great place for beautiful looking fonts. Ref: https://typekit.com (left) A free resource for nice looking web fonts. Ref: https://edgewebfonts.adobe.com (right)

Arial Black

Bookman

Garamond

Impact

Trebuchet MS

Avant Garde

Comic Sans MS

Georgia

Palatino

Verdana

CSS3 web fonts

CSS3 allows you to import your own fonts into a web page. This is amazing, as you are no longer bound by the limitations of the fonts that people have on their computers—you can just bring your own fonts to the website!

Before CSS3 web fonts, heading text would be created with image-editing programs such as Photoshop. Thankfully, CSS3 web fonts allows us to retire this process once and for all!

Serif, sans-serif, & monospace font families

These are the three basic font families: serif, sans-serif, and monotype. Serif-type fonts have a little line at the end of some characters (called a "serif"). Sans-serif fonts don't have this line. All the characters in monospace fonts have the same width.

Adding fonts

Adding fonts to a web page can be a bit involved, as there are several font formats—some browsers understand some, while other browsers only understand others. There are font converters out there that will make the necessary conversions, but there is also a much easier option in the form of Google Fonts.

Google Fonts are free, and using them really simplifies the process, as Google takes care of all the format conversions. It will even host the fonts for you, so you don't have to upload them to your web server. Here's how you add Google Fonts to your web pages.

1. Go to www.google.com/fonts. You will see a long list of fonts.

2. The top tabs on the page allow you to view the fonts in action, either in a word, a sentence, a paragraph, or in large "poster" format.

3. You can filter the fonts at the left by category and view them in a different format (bold, italic, and so on). Play around with the options when you get to the page to see how the fonts look with different settings applied.

4. Once you've found a font you like, click on the "quick use" button. This takes you to a page that shows the CSS link you will use in your website to include the font.

A close up view of some of the fonts at Google Fonts.

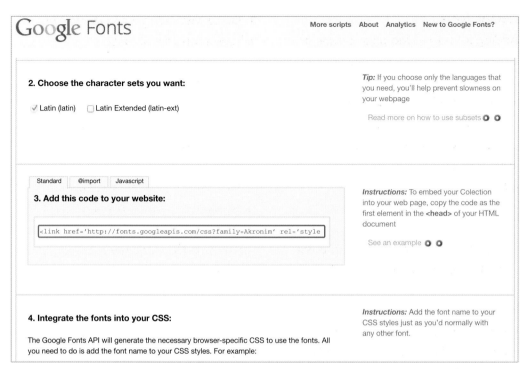

Google fonts—I've highlighted (with the red box) the CSS link you copy & paste into your web pages.

5. Add the font link to your pages (note that the specific link varies, depending on the font you choose). In this example, we linked to a Google Font called Akronim:

```
<link href='http://fonts.
googleapis.com/css?family=Akronim'
rel='stylesheet' type='text/css'>
```

6. You can now use your chosen Google Font in your web pages:

```
body {
font-family: 'Akronim', cursive;
}
```

There is more to learn about using web fonts, but most of you will be OK with the Google Fonts solution. If you want to learn more though, you can find a video tutorial at the book's website.

HTML5's new semantic tags

In Chapter 5 (pages 86–7) we discussed the semantic meaning of tags and even covered a few of the new HTML5 semantic tags. Let's take a closer look at these new semantic elements or tags (remember that tags are also known as "elements") to get a better idea how you can use them. First, here is a list of all the new HTML5 semantic tags:

```
<nav>
<footer>
<header>
<main>
<article>
<aside>
<details>
<figcaption>
<figure>
<mark>
<section>
<summary>
<time>
```

All the major browsers support (understand) the tags in this list, with the exception of the <main> tag in Internet Explorer 11 (and all earlier versions of the program). However, I will show you how to fix this.

As a reminder, these tags don't do anything in particular, other than provide meaning to the page and create a better structure. This is in contrast with, say, the <video> tag, which displays a fully capable video player in your web page.

Using the new semantic tags

Previously, when creating your page structure you have used <div> tags and then applied IDs to them such as "header," "footer," and so on. This is cool, but now you can just use the <header> and <footer> tags in their place. This also allows you to simplify your code. For example, you can take these <div>s:

```
<div id="header">
<p>header</p>
</div>
<div id="navigation">
<p>navigation</p>
</div>
<div id="centerDoc">
</div>
<!-- ends centerDoc-->
<div id="footer">
<p>footer</p>
</div>
```

And replace them like so:

```
<header>
<p>header</p>
</header>
<nav>
<p>navigation</p>
</nav>
<main>
<!-- replaces centerDoc-->
</main>
<footer>
<p>footer</p>
</footer>
```

Now that the tags are self-describing, you don't need to create IDs for them, so your CSS code can also be simplified. For example, this CSS code, which targets the ID "header:"

```
#header {
color: white;
}
```

Becomes this:

```
header {
color: white;
}
```

OK, this is not quite as big a difference as you saw with the HTML, but every little bit to simplify adds up.

Helping out IE8 and below

As I mentioned earlier, the number of people using IE8 and other older, less-capable browsers is falling fast. Therefore I am limiting my discussion on how to compensate for them to only the new HTML5 semantic tags or elements.

When IE8 and other older browsers don't recognize the new HTML5 semantic tags they consider them as inline tags. That causes the browser to display these tags all clumped-up, so everything appears squished up.

As you recall, block level tags are each rendered on their own line, with space between them and the tags that fall before and after. So, to fix the "squishing" problem, you simply have to add this line of CSS code:

```
article, aside, figure, caption,
figcaption, footer, header, main,
nav, section,
summary {
display: block;
}
```

This tells the browser to treat the tags as block tags, and problem solved! This CSS will have no effect on modern browsers that understand HTML5, as they already set these tags to block.

Final thoughts on HTML5 semantic tags

As you saw in the list on the previous page, there are many more semantic HTML5 tags that haven't gone into details about here, but we hit the big ones. More importantly, you now understand how to use them.

One final comment: <div> tags are still widely used today, especially when there isn't an HTML5 semantic tag replacement. For example, when you created the "container" <div> to center your page in Chapter 8, that's still the way to do it, there being no HTML5 "container" tag.

Ref: http://buongiorno.illy.com

These great looking websites would not be possible without heavy use of HTML5 and CSS3.

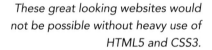

Ref: http://www.bottegaromana.fr

Ref: http://www.lighthousebrewing.com

CSS3 backgrounds

We've looked at using CSS to add images to web pages before, but traditional CSS methods are limited when it comes to full page background images. Let's first see what the problem is, and then I will show you how to solve it with a new CSS3 property: background-size.

About two months ago, I was walking through my local graveyard—it's an old graveyard that sits at the top of the mountain in my home town, Montreal. I came across this amazing Celtic cross headstone, and thought it would make a great background for a web page.

So, let's add the image to the background of a page:

```
body {
background: url("celtic-vampire.
png") no-repeat right top;
        background-size: cover;
}
```

If you look at the screenshot below (1), you see that the photo is getting cut off—it's just too big.

The original Celtic cross photo.

*The cover broken
(left) and fixed.*

Using CSS3 background-size

The ideal thing would be to have the background image scale with the web page. CSS3 background-size will do this:

```
body {
background: url("celtic-vampire.
png") no-repeat right top;
-webkit-background-size: cover;
-moz-background-size: cover;
-o-background-size: cover;
background-size: cover;
}
```

The key line of code is: "background-size: cover." You'll notice that I also have the same code with the prefixes:

```
-webkit-
-moz-
-o-
```

This makes the code work with older browser versions, although if you play with the browser window size, you may sometimes lose the full "cover" effect (2). You can fix this easily (3), by adding this CSS code in your <body> tag selector:

```
background-attachment: fixed;
```

So, the complete CSS code is:

```
body {
background: url("celtic-vampire.
png") no-repeat right top;
-webkit-background-size: cover;
-moz-background-size: cover;
-o-background-size: cover;
background-size: cover;
background-attachment: fixed;
}
```

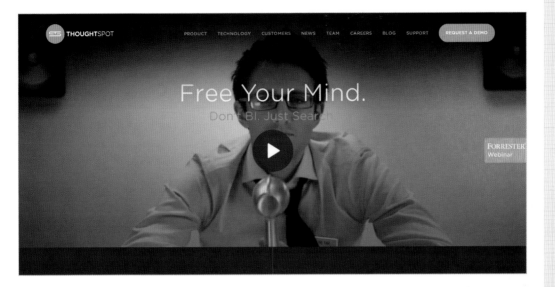

Cinemagraphs

In Chapter 5 I mentioned cinemagraphs. These are simply animated gif images that are used as background images for a web page (using background-size: cover). It creates a really cool effect that is almost like using a video for your web page's background. However, as animated gifs are relatively light files, they load fast.

It's hard to show you how an animated background looks in a printed book (and I would like you to see the effect) so instead, I've put a video tutorial on the book's website that you can refer to.

The full-screen video makes this largely black-and-white page look amazing. Ref: http://www.thoughtspot.com

Fullscreen background video

With the help of HTML5, you can use video for the background of web pages. Although this is super-cool, you only want to do this when it makes sense—that's when it serves the purpose of the site. You can learn how to do this at the book's website.

CSS media queries

One of the big challenges facing web designers these days is the fact that a lot of people are surfing the web on all kinds of different devices with different screen sizes (iPhones, iPads, Android Note 4, laptops, desktop PCs, and so on). This variety makes it hard to design a website that fits nicely on all these devices.

CSS media queries is new to CSS3. It allows you to detect the screen size of the device or computer that a website is being viewed on, so you can change your CSS and be sure that your pages fit properly for each particular user.

I showed you examples of this early on in the book: the screenshots below show how the layout of my video training site changes depending on the size of the browser window. This change in the page layout is, of course, all controlled by the CSS code. (Bootstrap uses media queries behind the scenes to help make this happen.)

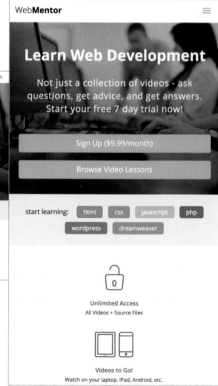

Webmentor.org uses media queries to help resize the video as the browser window changes size.
Ref: https://webmentor.org

You have two options for applying your media queries: you can either use media queries directly in your CSS code, or you can use media queries to direct the web browser to a specialized style sheet depending on the size of the screen the website is being viewed on.

1. CSS media query in code
Max-width
In the style sheet or CSS code in the <head> of your web page, add this code:

```
@media screen and (max-width:960px)
{
#container {
width:960px;
margin-top:10px;
}
}
@media screen and (max-width:560px)
{
#container {
width:560px;
margin-top:10px;
}
}
```

The important lines here have "@media" in them—this is the media query code.

The first query— @media screen and (max-width:960px)—says this is for any screen device. It then asks CSS to check if the screen width is up to 960px; if it is, the #container <div> is set to 960px.

The second media query— @media screen and (max-width:560px)—is looking for screen sizes with a maximum width of 560px. If it finds that the screen is indeed 560px or less, it makes the #container <div> 560px.

Min-width
You can also check screen size using min-width:

```
@media screen and (min-width:960px)
{
#container {
width:960px;
margin-top:10px;
}
}
```

In this example, if the screen size is at least 960px, the CSS code will apply.

Combining media queries

You can also combine media queries. The following CSS code will be applied if the screen size is between 600px and 960px.:

```
@media screen and (min-width:
600px) and (max-width: 960px)  {
#container {
width:960px;
color: red;
}
}
```

Device width

The code below will apply if the maximum device width is 667px, for example (the iPhone 6 display).

```
@media screen and (max-device-
width: 667px) {
.class {
background: #000;
}
}
```

CSS media query in CSS links

Another way to use media queries is to embed the query in your CSS link code. This way, you can have entire style sheets for each screen size—a better strategy as it allows you to keep your code better organized. For example, you would put this in your <head> tag:

What is the difference between max-width and max-device-width?

Max-width is the width of the target device's display area: the size of a browser window, for example. Max-device-width is the width of the target device's entire rendering area: the full screen area of a smartphone or computer monitor, for example.

Targeting different media types

The @media rule allows you to target different media types (screens or printed pages), so you can apply different CSS code. So if you wanted to change the color of your text in the page just for printing, you would use: @media print { /**css code in here**/}

```
<link rel="stylesheet"
media="screen and (max-width:
600px)" href="small-600.css" />
<link rel="stylesheet"
media="screen and (max-width:
960px)" href="big-960.css" />
```

Embedding video & audio into web pages

There a several ways to add or embed video into web pages:

- Using an external helper plugin app, such as Adobe Flash.

- Use the old-school <embed> tag (which is very limited).

- Use HTML5's <video> tag (which is the newest option).

Adobe Flash

I mentioned Flash very briefly earlier in the book and advised you not to learn it. However, using Flash for embedding video is a viable option, as 99% of all desktop and laptop computers have the Flash Player installed. Another advantage of using Flash for video is that it has a lot of controls and options that you don't have with the other two methods.

Downsides to Flash are that it can be a security risk and it's also a memory hog—meaning that it can use up all a computer's memory and cause it to crash, especially Macs. It's happened to me on many occasions!

The old style video embed—ouch!

The bigger downside is that iPhones and iPads will not run Flash-based video— Apple has disabled Flash on these devices for years. As a result, Flash on mobile is effectively dead.

The <embed> tag

Using the <embed> tag works, but it isn't the best option:

- You have no video controls. You can only start and stop a video by clicking on it, but there is nothing telling the user that!

Two custom HTML5 video players that are free to use.
Refs: http://www.jwplayer.com,
http://www.sublimevideo.net

- The web browser cannot display a preview image that looks any good.

- The user has to give permission to the browser to play the video. Until you do, you usually get an ugly-looking image where the video is supposed to play.

In a nutshell: don't use it! However, this is the <embed> tag in action, just so you can get a taste:

```
<embed id="video" src="birds-
flying-miami.mp4" width="834"
height="519">
```

When you use the <embed> tag, the browser will use the default video player on the computer to play back the video file—if it can.

The problem is, not all video formats can be played on all computers—the Windows WMV video format does not easily play back on Macs, for example. The solution is to use MP4 video, which can be played on all computers.

The HTML5 <video> tag

Going forward, this will be the way to embed video into web pages, but there is one issue: not all web browsers can play all the video types. The HTML5 video player supports (can play back) a few different types:

- MP4
- WebM
- Ogg

Why are there so many video types? There are lots of reasons—some legal, some technical, and some are simply because nerds like to do things their own way! All you need to know is that all modern browsers can play back MP4 video, with the exception of Opera (and as Opera has only 1% of the market share, this is not a major concern).

Video fallback options

If you are worried that people using Opera and some older browsers will have problems with video, there are fallback methods you can use if the HTML5 doesn't work. In fact, there are a few options out there—just use one of the many free HTML5 video players that will take care of all the dirty details for you. Here is a small selection:

VideoJS (http://www.videojs.com)
JWplayer (http://www.jwplayer.com)
Sublime Video Player
(http://www.sublimevideo.net)

However, this is a problem that is going away fast as the browser makers get up to speed and stop bickering over how to play video. Using the HTML5 player itself should be pretty safe going forward, but you should always test your code, especially if you find yourself in a situation where you need to support a really old web browser.

Default video players

On Windows the default video player is Windows Media Player; the Mac default is Quicktime.

Using the HTML5 <video> tag

Now that nerd-chatter is out of the way, let's embed some video using the HTML5 <video> tag:

```
<video poster="birds-flying.
png" controls loop width="834"
height="519">
<source src="birds-flying-miami.mp4"
type="video/mp4">
<source src="birds-flying-miami.
webm" type="video/webm">
<p>Your browser sucks! So you can't
see the video. Upgrade, the 1990s
are long gone! :)</p>
</video>
```

Let's go over the line of code for the <video> tag. First the attributes:

- **poster:** This is like a movie poster—it allows you to set an image that is displayed before the video is started.
- **controls:** Displays video controllers.
- **loop:** Tells the browser whether to loop the video or not.
- **width and height:** Sets the dimensions of the video.

Video embedded with the default HTML5 video player.

There are other attribute options available for the <video> tag:

- **autoplay:** Tells the browser to start playing the video automatically.
- **muted:** Turn off the sound.
- **preload:** Preloads the video.

The preload attribute has further options:

- **preload="none":** tells the browser not to preload the video.
- **preload="auto":** tells the browser to start preloading the video as soon as the page is loaded.
- **preload="metadata":** tells the browser to load the metadata about the video. Metadata is extra information about the video, such as its name, size, duration, and so on.

The <source> sub tag allows you to specify the video location, name, and type. In the example on the previous page I have used the same video, but encoded two different formats. The first is the MP4 version for modern browsers, but as a fallback I also included the location for a WebM version of this video for Opera. So when Opera comes across the <video> tag, it will skip the MP4 version and load the WebM version instead.

Finally, you may have noticed that I added this paragraph:

```
<p>Your browser sucks! So you can't
see the video. Upgrade, the 1990s
are long gone! :)</p>
```

This is for really, really old browsers who don't understand the <video> tag. They will just skip the <video> tag and its sub tags, until the browser hits the <p> tag, which it will display instead.

Alternatively, you could embed a video that you have uploaded to YouTube. Again, this is another fallback that is quickly becoming less necessary, but here's the code for embedding a video from YouTube:

```
<video poster="birds-flying.
png" controls loop width="834"
height="519">
<source src="birds-flying-miami.mp4"
type="video/mp4">
<source src="birds-flying-miami.
webm" type="video/webm">
<iframe width="640" height="360"
src="//www.youtube.com/embed/
dvJr3a9WztM" frameborder="0"
allowfullscreen></iframe>
</video>
```

Embedding audio

Embedding audio is pretty much a mirror of embedding video with regards to players, embedding options, and so on. Again, the Opera web browser is the only one that doesn't support the most popular format (in the case of audio this is MP3), although it does support the opensource Ogg format, and the Windows WAV format.

Let's look at the <audio> tag in action:

```
<audio controls>
<source src="opera-comments.ogg"
type="audio/ogg">
<source src="opera-comments.mp3"
type="audio/mpeg">
Your browser does not support the
audio element.
</audio>
```

As with the <video> tag, the web browser will look at the <source> tags and use the media type that it understands. In this case it will be either the Ogg audio file or the MP3 file.

The HTML5 audio player embedded at the top of a page, using default controls.

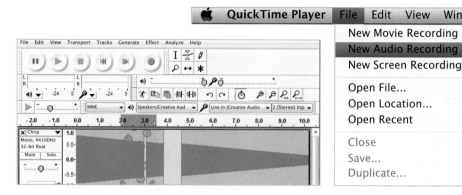

Audacity on Windows.   Quicktime on Mac.

The <audio> tag supports many of the same attributes of <video> tag:

- autoplay
- controls
- loop
- muted
- preload
- src

Since you are now experts at the <video> tag, no point in wasting paper describing the same options!

Converting audio formats

There are numerous options if you want to convert your sound files to MP3. If you have WAV files, then perhaps the easiest option is Apple's free iTunes software: it's available for both Mac and Windows and will allow you to convert WAV files to the MP3 format.

If you need a more flexible solution you will find there are many websites and free apps that will convert different file types to MP3 or Ogg; search online for "convert MP3 to Ogg," "convert WAV to MP3," or whatever other conversion your require.

Recording audio

I am not going to get into much detail here, as this not an audio recording book, but it is worth noting that there are many free options out there when it comes to recording audio on a computer. Apple's Quicktime player has the ability to record audio, for example, as does Audacity. This is a popular and free app for Windows and Mac OS that not only records audio, but also provides almost pro-level editing and output options.

CSS3 special effects

We are going to close off this monster chapter with a look at some cool CSS3 special effects. Prior to CSS3 these are things that web designers could only do with the help of images and sometimes complex trickery. Rejoice—you are learning this stuff at the right time!

Rounded corners with: border-radius

You can easily create rounded borders using the border-radius property (1).

The code you need is:

```
p {
border-radius: 25px;
}
```

In this example the 25px defines how rounded the corners are. You can change the shape of the corners like so (2):

```
p {
border-radius: 10em 25px;
}
```

Rounded corners with border-radius.

Rounded corners affecting the shape.

Background shadow with: box-shadow

You can also add box shadows to any element as well. In this example (3) the shadow is white—go figure! The code:

```
p {
box-shadow: 10px 10px 25px #FFF;
}
```

The first number (10px) sets the shadow's horizontal position, the second number its vertical and the third number sets the spread (how spread-out the shadow is). The last value is, of course, the color of the shadow.

Transparency with: opacity

You guessed it! We can make elements on the page transparent with very little code (4):

```
p {
opacity: 0.7;
}
```

The opacity range controls transparency, and goes from 0 (fully transparent) to 1 (fully opaque). Here, the value is set to 0.7, which gives 30% transparency. If you were to set it to 0.2, it would be 80% transparent. Makes sense?

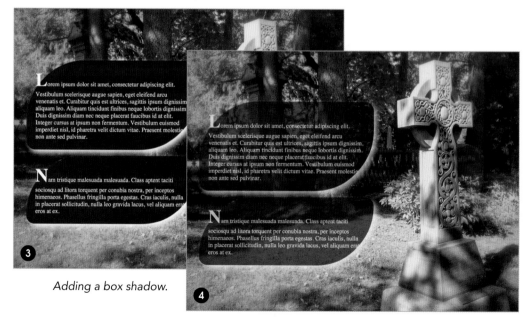

Adding a box shadow.

Making our <p> semi transparent.

Gradients with linear-gradient

CSS3 gradients allow you to display transitions between two or more specified colors (5). There are two types of gradient: linear and radial. Here's the code to add a linear gradient:

```
p {
background: linear-gradient(white,
black);
}
```

And here's a radial gradient (6):

```
p {
background: radial-gradient(white,
green, black)
}
```

Where to learn more

There are many more special effects in CSS3. I've put a few video lessons for you on this—and other HTML5 goodies—on the book's website, and you can also learn more here: http://www.w3schools.com/css/css3_intro.asp.

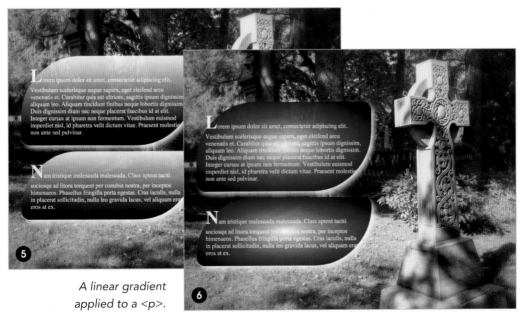

A linear gradient applied to a <p>.

A radial gradient applied to a <p>.

CHAPTER 12

Introduction to jQuery & Bootstrap

Earlier in the book I mentioned web frameworks and libraries. Well, you've come a long way since then, so you are now ready to take your first peek at (arguably) the two most important ones out there: jQuery and Bootstrap.

First, you are going to get a feel for the position of jQuery within the web design world. Then you will learn how to install and use it in your websites.

After jQuery, you will go over Bootstrap in the same way!

This Swiss site uses of jQuery to help create great looking animations. Ref: http://captormania.migros.ch

BOOTSTRAP		
HTML5	CSS3	JQUERY
HTML	CSS	JAVASCRIPT
WEB BROWSER		

How jQuery and Bootstrap fit into the web design technology stack.

A quick look at jQuery

You can't expect to become a jQuery master in a beginner's web design book, so the aim here is to provide you with a quick overview, so that you come away with a basic understanding of what it is and how to use it.

What exactly is jQuery?

jQuery is a JavaScript library that makes using JavaScript much easier. It also provides lots of effects, such as faders, sliders, that even nonprogrammers can use in their web pages. jQuery is so powerful that many popular web frameworks use it behind the scenes, such as AngularJS, EmberJS, Bootstrap, CSS grids, Modernizr, and Underscore.js

Does a web designer need to learn all the different frameworks?

The short answer is "no." You will see frameworks come and go—there are many out there! It's good to keep your eye on them, but working web designers generally need to be picky about adopting new technologies.

to name just a few. Even though jQuery is not part of the official web specification and is not built into web browsers, it is still a fundamental tool in web design today.

jQuery.com is the place to go to download the latest version.

Installing jQuery

To install jQuery you have two options: either download the jQuery library to your website, or better, just link to the jQuery library from a CDN. What's a CDN? CDN is short for "Content Delivery Network," which is a website that acts as a host for content (which in this case is jQuery). Google and Microsoft act as CDNs and so you know the jQuery files will likely always be there.

The use of CDNs is becoming more and more common because it provides two advantages. First, you don't have to bother downloading and installing things. Second, with a popular library like jQuery, it's likely users may have downloaded it from a CDN when visiting other sites. This means when they come to you, jQuery will already be installed and ready to go. This will lead to your website loading faster.

What's the <script> tag?

The <script> tag (as seen in the code to the right) is used to link to external JavaScript files, just like the <link> tag is used to link to external CSS files.

You can download jQuery at http://jQuery.com, but my suggestion is to just use a CDN.

Getting jQuery on your web page

For the example that follows I will be using the Google CDN to load jQuery. Therefore, in the <head> of your page, you will need to add a link to the jQuery library that Google is hosting:

```
<head>
<script src="http://ajax.
googleapis.com/ajax/libs/
/1.11.1/jQuery.min.js»></script>
</head>
```

Now that you have jQuery hooked up to your page, you can start using it. Let's look at a super-simple example where we use jQuery to make a paragraph disappear when someone clicks on a button.

Check out this code:

```
<!DOCTYPE html>
<html>
<head>
<script src="http://ajax.
googleapis.com/ajax/
libs/jQuery/1.11.1/jQuery.min.
js"></script>
```

```
<script>
$(document).ready(function(){
  $("button").click(function(){
    $("p").hide();
  });
});
</script>
</head>
<body>

<h1>Let's make the paragraphs
disappear!</h1>
<p>This is a paragraph.</p>
<p>Lorem ipsum dolor sit amet,
consectetur adipiscing elit.
Mauris metus urna, fringilla nec
sollicitudin id, condimentum ac
velit. Sed dictum nunc et neque
bibendum, id iaculis magna gravida.
Sed a finibus lorem. Aenean
```

```
tincidunt, ante at convallis
hendrerit, nulla diam tempus metus,
et porttitor tellus lectus at
nulla. Nam ac urna sapien. Proin
scelerisque consequat massa, ac
ornare dui varius consequat.
Donec non tempus sapien. </p>
<button>Click me</button>

</body>
</html>
```

Why would you want to make a <p> disappear? This is a simple example, but making tags appear and disappear on the page (as in 1 and 2) is the basis of fancy menu systems and other user interface wizardry. The point is to show you how easy jQuery makes this.

Let's make the paragraphs disappear!

Lorem ipsum dolor sit amet, consectetur adipiscing elit. Mauris metes uma, fringilla nee sollicitudi condimentum ac velit. S. dictum none et neque bibendum, id iaculis magna gravida. S. a fmibus lor Aenean tincidunt, ante at convallis hendrerit, nulls diam tempos metes, et poMitor tellus lectus at n uma sapien. Proin scelerisque consequat massa, ac omare dui varies consequat. Donee non tempus

This is another paragraph.

Click me

❶

Let's make the paragraphs disappear!

Click me

❷

jQuery makes all the <p>s disappear!

Most of this code is pretty standard stuff, the only thing that we will need to talk about are these lines:

```
<script>
$(document).ready(function(){
    $("button").click(function(){
        $("p").hide();
    });
});
</script>
```

First, if you are going to have JavaScript or jQuery code in your page, you need to use the opening and closing <script> tags (3). Like any other tags, the closing script tag (</script>) has a forward-leaning slash prepending it. This line:

```
$(document).ready(function(){
```

... tells the web browser to wait until the whole page is loaded before doing anything. You want to do this to prevent

your code from trying to do stuff before the page loads—otherwise it could break the code. The next line:

```
$("button").click(function(){
```

... is actually doing two things. First it is targeting the <button> tag on the page. This is similar to using CSS to target tags, only now this code is targeting the button for jQuery, not for CSS. Second, the code:

```
.click(function){
```

... is saying: when someone clicks on the button, do this. So anything between this code block gets run:

```
$(document).ready(function(){
```

This is the code that is run when someone clicks on the button.

```
});
```

```
 4   <script src="http://ajax.googleapis.com/ajax/libs/jquery/1.11.1/
     script>
 5
 6   <script>
 7
 8   $(document).ready(function(){        ◄———— Opening code block
 9
10       $("button").click(function(){
11           $("p").hide();
12       });
13
14   });                                  ◄———— Closing code block
15
16   </script>
17   </head>
18   <body>
```

3

Finally, you are simply getting jQuery to make all the <p> disappear with this line of code:

```
$("p").hide();
```

Finishing up with jQuery

jQuery is a big library with a lot of capability. Though it is important that you understand the basics it is not essential that you become a jQuery expert to be an amazing web designer.

But if you are interested in learning more, check out the book's website where I will point you to more resources.

jQuery UI

jQuery has a library of components that are divided into four sections:
1. Interactions
2. Widgets
3. Effects
4. Utilities
You can simply grab these code chunks and drop them into your site. For me, the most important is the date picker component. To use the date picker, you just need to add this script code to the head of your web page:

```
<script>
$(function() {
$( "#datepicker" ).datepicker();
});
</script>
```

Then you need to add the id "datepicker" to the form input tag that you want to transform into a date picker:

```
<input type="text"
id="datepicker">
```

You can check out all the jQuery UI components at: http://jqueryui.com.

A brief introduction to Bootstrap

Bootstrap is an HTML, CSS, and JavaScript framework that is designed to make building responsive websites much easier.

As you recall, a responsive website adapts to the device so that it resizes, and will even move page elements around to best fit the screen. Bootstrap goes a long way to making this relatively easy.

The website getbootstrap.com is the home of Bootstrap.

Installing Bootstrap

As with jQuery, you could download all the files, or you could use a CDN:

```
<link rel="stylesheet"
href="http://maxcdn.bootstrapcdn.
com/bootstrap/3.2.0/css/bootstrap.
min.css">
```

Sonce you are probably comfortable now looking at code, here is the complete Bootstrap-ready page—pay attention to what's in the <head> and what's at the bottom of the page:

```
<!DOCTYPE html>
<html>
<head>
<meta name="viewport"
content="width=device-width,
initial-scale=1">
<link rel="stylesheet"
href="http://maxcdn.bootstrapcdn.
com/bootstrap/3.2.0/css/bootstrap.
min.css">
</head>
<body>
<script src="https://ajax.
googleapis.com/ajax/
libs/jQuery/1.11.1/jQuery.min.js">
</script>
<script src="http://maxcdn.
bootstrapcdn.com/bootstrap/3.2.0/
js/bootstrap.min.js"></script>
</body>
</html>
```

You will notice that besides the link to the Bootstrap CSS (using a CDN) in the <head>, there is also a link to the

Bootstrap grid examples

Basic grid layouts to get you familiar with building within the Bootstrap grid system.

Three equal columns

Get three equal-width columns **starting at desktops and scaling to larger desktops**. On mobile devices, tablets and below, the columns will automatically stack.

| .col-md-4 | .col-md-4 | .col-md-4 |

Three unequal columns

Get three columns **starting at desktops and scaling to larger desktops** of various widths. Remember, grid columns should add up to twelve for a single horizontal block. More than that and columns start stacking no matter the viewport.

| .col-md-3 | .col-md-6 | .col-md-3 |

Two columns

Get two columns **starting at desktops and scaling to larger desktops.**

Bootstrap JavaScript library (bootstrap.min.js) and the jQuery library (jQuery.min.js). This will give you everything you need to use Bootstrap!

The Bootstrap framework has all kinds of components that you can just drop into your websites, such as buttons, drop-down menus, icon sets, customized form elements, and more, but I think the coolest thing about it is the grid-based layout system. By using the Bootstrap grid structure for page layouts, your sites will automatically work on all devices— from smartphones to desktop computers with 27-inch monitors.

How does the Bootstrap grid work?
In a nutshell, Bootstrap has a bunch of CSS classes that you apply to your web page according to the defined Bootstrap HTML structure; you have to know how to use the <div>s properly, but it's actually

pretty easy. Doing this will allow you to easily create all kinds of layout styles/ structures that will work in all the web browsers and on any sized device—the Bootstrap framework takes care of a lot of the details for you.

A quick example of Bootstrap's grid
To finish off this quick look at Bootstrap, I want to give you an example of the grid system in action. First, here's the code (see 1 and 2 on the following page to see how it looks):

```
<div class=»container»>
<h1>Hello World!</h1>
<p>Resize the browser window to
see the effect.</p>
<div class="row">
<div class="col-sm-4"
style="background-color:lavender;">
<!-- Using Bootstrap Utility Class
-->
```

```
<h1 class="visible-lg">The Screen
is Big!</h1>
<p>1. Lorem ipsum dolor sit amet,
consectetur adipisicing elit, sed
do eiusmod tempor incididunt ut
labore et dolore magna aliqua.</p>
</div>

<div class="col-sm-8"
style="background-
color:lavenderblush;">
<p>2. Sed ut perspiciatis unde
omnis iste natus error sit
voluptatem accusantium doloremque
laudantium, totam rem aperiam,
eaque ipsa quae ab illo inventore
veritatis et quasi architecto
beatae vitae dicta sunt
explicabo.</p>
</div>
</div>
```

In the code you will notice that there are <div>s tagged with specific classes: container, row, col-sm-4, and col-sm-8. These are a few examples of the many predefined Bootstrap classes that make the layout magic happen. By applying these classes in the right ways, your pages will come together and work flawlessly.

Bootstrap utility classes

Bootstrap has utility CSS classes that can show and hide elements in the page, based on the screen size. Check out this line of code and the effect it has (3):

```
<h1 class="visible-lg">The Screen
is Big!</h1>
```

Hello World!

Resize the browser window to see the effect.

1. Lorem ipsum dolor sit amet, consectetur adipiscing elit, sed do eiusmod tempod incidunt ut labore et dolore magna aliqua.

2. Sed ut perspiciatis unde omnis iste natus error sit accusantium doloremque laudantium, totam rem ap ab illo inventore veritatis et quasi architecto beatae expilacbo.

Hello World!

Resize the browser window to see the effect.

1. Lorem ipsum dolor sit amet, consectetur adipiscing elit, sed do eiusmod tempod incidunt ut labore et dolore magna aliqua.

2. Sed ut perspiciatis unde omnis iste natus error sit voluptatem accusantium doloremque laudantium, totam rem aperiam, eaque ipsa quae ab illo inventore veritatis et quasi architecto beatae vutae dicta sunt expilacbo.

The Bootstrap grid system automatically stacking <div>s as the page is resized.

Hello World!

Resize the browser window to see the effect.

The Screen is Big!

1. Lorem ipsum dolor sit amet, consectetur adipiscing elit, sed do eiusmod tempod incidunt ut labore et dolore magna aliqua.

2. Sed ut perspiciatis unde omnis iste natus error sit voluptatem accusantium doloremaperiam, eaque ipsa quae ab illo inventore veritatis et quasi architecto beatae

Bootstrap's utility class used to make text appear when the browser. window is resized to a particular size.

Notice the "visible-lg" class. This is an example of a Bootstrap utility class. In this instance, it will cause the <h1> to only appear when the display/screen is large—1170px or bigger. This is just one tool that saves you from having to do a lot of extra work to get your layout to fit mobile devices and desktop computers at the same time.

Finishing up with Bootstrap

As with jQuery, we've only scratched the surface of Bootstrap—again, whole books have been written about it. You can learn more about Bootstrap at getbootstrap. com/getting-started/, and I will also be posting more information on this book's website, at www.webdesignstarthere.com.

We're at the end! Some final comments...

Yes, we've come to an end with this book, but you have only just begun! As I am sure you've figured out by now, web design is a big field, with lots to learn!

However, you are now armed with a good foundation that you can build on— quite literally, as your next step is to start building websites. And with each one you complete your skills will sharpen, and you will slowly develop the "nerd-eyes" that allow you to see things a little more clearly than you do now.

You should also continue to learn more, diving deeper into jQuery and Bootstrap, for example, and exploring more HTML5 and CSS3. You might even get into server-side programming a little bit, with PHP, or Ruby, or Python perhaps. Either way, the more you learn, the more you will earn.

Thanks for reading!
—Stefan

Index

Acknowledgments

First, I should thank Ilex for giving me the opportunity to write my first book! Though I have been writing for years on my blogs, and occasionally for magazines, the process of writing a book has challenged me on whole new level. This experience has raised my game overall, and that alone was reason enough to take on the job.

It's always good to do new things.

I should also thank everyone at Ilex who helped me with the book, including Kate Haynes and Frank Gallaugher, but with special thanks to my editor Alannah Moore—she made the job much easier.

Like everyone else who has had the opportunity to pen a book, I appreciate the words of encouragement from friends and family.

—Stefan